GRADE 7

Mindset Mathematics

Visualizing and Investigating Big Ideas

Jo Boaler

Jen Munson

Cathy Williams

JB JOSSEY-BASS™

A Wiley Brand

Published by Jossey-Bass
A Wiley Brand
535 Mission Street, 14th Floor, San Francisco, CA 94105-3253—www.josseybass.com

Jossey-Bass books and products are available through most bookstores. To contact Jossey-Bass directly call our Customer Care Department within the U.S. at 800-956-7739, outside the U.S. at 317-572-3986, or fax 317-572-4002.

Wiley publishes in a variety of print and electronic formats and by print-on-demand. Some material included with standard print versions of this book may not be included in e-books or in print-on-demand. If this book refers to media such as a CD or DVD that is not included in the version you purchased, you may download this material at http://booksupport.wiley.com. For more information about Wiley products, visit www.wiley.com.

The Visualize, Play, and Investigate icons are used under license from Shutterstock.com and the following arists: Blan-k, Marish, and SuzanaM.

Library of Congress Cataloging-in-Publication Data

Names: Boaler, Jo, 1964- author. | Munson, Jen, 1977- author. | Williams,
    Cathy, 1962- author.
Title: Mindset mathematics : visualizing and investigating big ideas, grade 7
    / Jo Boaler, Jen Munson, Cathy Williams.
Description: San Francisco : Jossey-Bass, [2019] | Includes index.
Identifiers: LCCN 2019016704 (print) | LCCN 2019018526 (ebook) | ISBN
    9781119357971 (Adobe PDF) | ISBN 9781119358015 (ePub) | ISBN 9781119357919
    (pbk.)
Subjects: LCSH: Games in mathematics education. | Mathematics—Study and
    teaching (Middle school)—Activity programs. | Seventh grade (Education)
Classification: LCC QA20.G35 (ebook) | LCC QA20.G35 B637 2019 (print) | DDC
    510.71/2—dc23
LC record available at https://lccn.loc.gov/2019016704

Cover design by Wiley
Cover image: © Marish/Shutterstock-Eye; © Kritchanut/iStockphoto- Background
Printed in the United States of America

FIRST EDITION

PB Printing   V10011982_070519

Contents

To all those teachers pursuing a mathematical mindset journey with us.

Introduction

I still remember the moment when Youcubed, the Stanford center I direct, was conceived. I was at the Denver NCSM and NCTM conferences in 2013, and I had arranged to meet Cathy Williams, the director of mathematics for Vista Unified School District. Cathy and I had been working together for the past year improving mathematics teaching in her district. We had witnessed amazing changes taking place, and a filmmaker had documented some of the work. I had recently released my online teacher course, called How to Learn Math, and been overwhelmed by requests from tens of thousands of teachers to provide them with more of the same ideas. Cathy and I decided to create a website and use it to continue sharing the ideas we had used in her district and that I had shared in my online class. Soon after we started sharing ideas on the Youcubed website, we were invited to become a Stanford University center, and Cathy became the codirector of the center with me.

In the months that followed, with the help of one of my undergraduates, Montse Cordero, our first version of youcubed.org was launched. By January 2015, we had managed to raise some money and hire engineers, and we launched a revised version of the site that is close to the site you may know today. We were very excited that in the first month of that relaunch, we had five thousand visits to the site. At the time of writing this, we are now getting three million visits to the site each month. Teachers are excited to learn about the new research and to take the tools, videos, and activities that translate research ideas into practice and use them in their teaching.

Low-Floor, High-Ceiling Tasks

One of the most popular articles on our website is called "Fluency without Fear." I wrote this with Cathy when I heard from many teachers that they were being made to use timed tests in the elementary grades. At the same time, new brain science was emerging showing that when people feel stressed—as students do when facing a timed test—part of their brain, the working memory, is restricted. The working memory is exactly the area of the brain that comes into play when students need to calculate with math facts, and this is the exact area that is impeded when students are stressed. We have evidence now that suggests strongly that timed math tests in the early grades are responsible for the early onset of math anxiety for many students. I teach an undergraduate class at Stanford, and many of the undergraduates are math traumatized. When I ask them what happened to cause this, almost all of them will recall, with startling clarity, the time in elementary school when they were given timed tests. We are really pleased that "Fluency without Fear" has now been used across the United States to pull timed tests out of school districts. It has been downloaded many thousands of times and used in state and national hearings.

One of the reasons for the amazing success of the paper is that it does not just share the brain science on the damage of timed tests but also offers an alternative to timed tests: activities that teach math facts conceptually and through activities that students and teachers enjoy. One of the activities—a game called How Close to 100—became so popular that thousands of teachers tweeted photos of their students playing the game. There was so much attention on Twitter and other media that Stanford noticed and decided to write a news story on the damage of speed to mathematics learning. This was picked up by news outlets across the United States, including *US News & World Report,* which is part of the reason the white paper has now had so many downloads and so much impact. Teachers themselves caused this mini revolution by spreading news of the activities and research.

How Close to 100 is just one of many tasks we have on youcubed.org that are extremely popular with teachers and students. All our tasks have the feature of being "low floor and high ceiling," which I consider to be an extremely important quality for engaging all students in a class. If you are teaching only one student, then a mathematics task can be fairly narrow in terms of its content and difficulty. But whenever you have a group of students, there will be differences in their needs, and they will be challenged by different ideas. A low-floor, high-ceiling task is one in which everyone can engage, no matter what his or her prior understanding or knowledge, but also one that is open enough to extend to high levels, so that all students can be deeply challenged. In the last two years, we have launched an introductory week of mathematics lessons on our site that are open, visual, and low floor, high ceiling. These have been extremely popular with teachers; they have had approximately four million downloads and are used in 20% of schools across the United States.

In our extensive work with teachers around the United States, we are continually asked for more tasks that are like those on our website. Most textbook publishers seem to ignore or be unaware of research on mathematics learning, and most textbook questions are narrow and insufficiently engaging for students. It is imperative that the new knowledge of the ways our brains learn mathematics is incorporated into the lessons students are given in classrooms. It is for this reason that we chose to write a series of books that are organized around a principle of active student engagement, that reflect the latest brain science on learning, and that include activities that are low floor and high ceiling.

Youcubed Summer Camp

We recently brought 81 students onto the Stanford campus for a Youcubed summer math camp, to teach them in the ways that are encouraged in this book. We used open, creative, and visual math tasks. After only 18 lessons with us, the students improved their test score performance by an average of 50%, the equivalent of 1.6 years of school. More important, they changed their relationship with mathematics and started believing in their own potential. They did this, in part, because we talked to them about the brain science showing that

- There is no such thing as a math person—anyone can learn mathematics to high levels.
- Mistakes, struggle, and challenge are critical for brain growth.
- Speed is unimportant in mathematics.
- Mathematics is a visual and beautiful subject, and our brains want to think visually about mathematics.

All of these messages were key to the students' changed mathematics relationship, but just as critical were the tasks we worked on in class. The tasks and the messages about the brain were perfect complements to each other, as we told students they could learn anything, and we showed them a mathematics that was open, creative, and engaging. This approach helped them see that they could learn mathematics and actually do so. This book shares the kinds of tasks that we used in our summer camp, that make up our week of inspirational mathematics (WIM) lessons, and that we post on our site.

Before I outline and introduce the different sections of the book and the ways we are choosing to engage students, I will share some important ideas about how students learn mathematics.

Memorization versus Conceptual Engagement

Many students get the wrong idea about mathematics—exactly the wrong idea. Through years of mathematics classes, many students come to believe that their role in mathematics learning is to memorize methods and facts, and that mathematics success comes from memorization. I say this is exactly the wrong idea because there is actually very little to remember in mathematics. The subject is made up of a few big, linked ideas, and students who are successful in mathematics are those who see the subject as a set of ideas that they need to think deeply about. The Program for International Student Assessment (PISA) tests are international assessments of mathematics, reading, and science that are given every three years. In 2012, PISA not only assessed mathematics achievement but also collected data on students' approach to mathematics. I worked with the PISA team in Paris at the Organisation for Economic Co-operation and Development (OECD) to analyze students' mathematics approaches and their relationship to achievement. One clear result emerged from this analysis. Students approached mathematics in three distinct ways. One group approached mathematics by attempting to memorize the methods they had met; another group took a "relational" approach, relating new concepts to those they already knew; and a third group took a self-monitoring approach, thinking about what they knew and needed to know.

In every country, the memorizers were the lowest-achieving students, and countries with high numbers of memorizers were all lower achieving. In no country were memorizers in the highest-achieving group, and in some high-achieving countries such as Japan, students who combined self-monitoring and relational strategies outscored memorizing students by more than a year's worth of schooling. More detail on this finding is given in this *Scientific American* Mind article that I coauthored with a PISA analyst: https://www.scientificamerican.com/article/ why-math-education-in-the-u-s-doesn-t-add-up/.

Mathematics is a conceptual subject, and it is important for students to be thinking slowly, deeply, and conceptually about mathematical ideas, not racing through methods that they try to memorize. One reason that students need to think conceptually has to do with the ways the brain processes mathematics. When we learn new mathematical ideas, they take up a large space in our brain as the brain works out where they fit and what they connect with. But with time, as we move on with our understanding, the knowledge becomes compressed in the brain, taking up a very small space. For first graders, the idea of addition takes up a large space in their brains as they think about how it works and what it means, but for adults the idea of addition is compressed, and it takes up a small space. When adults are asked to add 2 and 3, for example, they can quickly and easily extract the compressed knowledge. William Thurston (1990), a mathematician who won the Field's Medal—the highest honor in mathematics—explains compression like this:

> Mathematics is amazingly compressible: you may struggle a long time, step by step, to work through the same process or idea from several approaches. But once you really understand it and have the mental perspective to see it as a whole, there is often a tremendous mental compression. You can file it away, recall it quickly and completely when you need it, and use it as just one step in some other mental process. The insight that goes with this compression is one of the real joys of mathematics.

You will probably agree with me that not many students think of mathematics as a "real joy," and part of the reason is that they are not compressing mathematical ideas in their brain. This is because the brain only compresses concepts, not methods. So if students are thinking that mathematics is a set of methods to memorize, they are on the wrong pathway, and it is critical that we change that. It is very important that students think deeply and conceptually about ideas. We provide the activities in this book that will allow students to think deeply and conceptually, and an essential role of the teacher is to give the students time to do so.

Mathematical Thinking, Reasoning, and Convincing

When we worked with our Youcubed camp students, we gave each of them journals to record their mathematical thinking. I am a big fan of journaling—for myself and my students. For mathematics students, it helps show them that mathematics is a subject for which we should record ideas and pictures. We can use journaling to encourage students to keep organized records, which is another important part of mathematics, and help them understand that mathematical thinking can be a long and slow process. Journals also give students free space—where they can be creative, share ideas, and feel ownership of their work. We did not write in the students' journals, as we wanted them to think of the journals as their space, not something that teachers wrote on. We gave students feedback on sticky notes that we stuck onto their work. The images in Figure I.1 show some of the mathematical records the camp students kept in their journals.

Another resource I always share with learners is the act of color coding—that is, students using colors to highlight different ideas. For example, when working on an algebraic task, they may show the x in the same color in an expression, in a graph, and in a picture, as shown in Figure I.2. When adding numbers, color coding may help show the addends (Figure I.3).

Color coding highlights connections, which are a really critical part of mathematics.

Another important part of mathematics is the act of reasoning—explaining why methods are chosen and how steps are linked, and using logic to connect ideas.

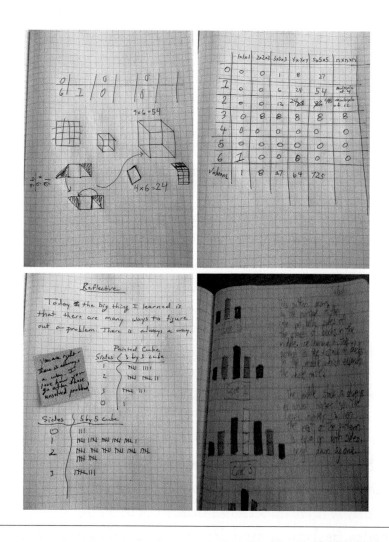

Figure I.1

Mindset Mathematics, Grade 7

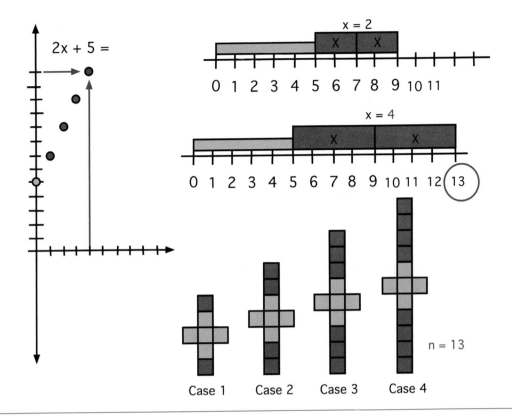

Figure I.2

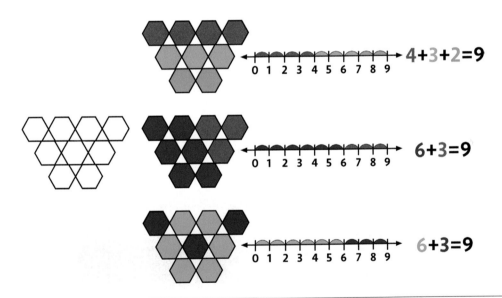

Figure I.3

Reasoning is at the heart of mathematics. Scientists prove ideas by finding more cases that fit a theory, or countercases that contradict a theory, but mathematicians prove their work by reasoning. If students are not reasoning, then they are not really doing mathematics. In the activities of these books, we suggest a framework that encourages students to be convincing when they reason. We tell them that there are three levels of being convincing. The first, or easiest, level is to convince yourself of something. A higher level is to convince a friend. And the highest level of all is to convince a skeptic. We also share with students that they should be skeptics with one another, asking one another why methods were chosen and how they work. We have found this framework to be very powerful with students; they enjoy being skeptics, pushing each other to deeper levels of reasoning, and it encourages students to reason clearly, which is important for their learning.

We start each book in our series with an activity that invites students to reason about mathematics and be convincing. I first met an activity like this when reading Mark Driscoll's teaching ideas in his book *Fostering Algebraic Thinking*. I thought it was a perfect activity for introducing the skeptics framework that I had learned from a wonderful teacher, Cathy Humphreys. She had learned about and adapted the framework from two of my inspirational teachers from England: mathematician John Mason and mathematics educator Leone Burton. As well as encouraging students to be convincing, in a number of activities we ask students to prove an idea. Some people think of proof as a formal set of steps that they learned in geometry class. But the act of proving is really about connecting ideas, and as students enter the learning journey of proving, it is worthwhile celebrating their steps toward formal proof. Mathematician Paul Lockhart (2012) rejects the idea that proving is about following a set of formal steps, instead proposing that proving is "abstract art, pure and simple. And art is always a struggle. There is no systematic way of creating beautiful and meaningful paintings or sculptures, and there is also no method for producing beautiful and meaningful mathematical arguments" (p. 8). Instead of suggesting that students follow formal steps, we invite them to think deeply about mathematical concepts and make connections. Students will be given many ways to be creative when they prove and justify, and for reasons I discuss later, we always encourage and celebrate visual as well as numerical and algebraic justifications. Ideally, students will create visual, numerical, and algebraic representations and connect their ideas through color coding and through verbal explanations. Students are excited to experience mathematics in these ways, and they benefit from the opportunity to bring their individual ideas and creativity to the problem-solving and learning space. As students develop in their mathematical understanding, we can encourage them to extend and generalize their ideas through reasoning, justifying, and proving. This process deepens their understanding and helps them compress their learning.

Big Ideas

The books in the Mindset Mathematics Series are all organized around mathematical "big ideas." Mathematics is not a set of methods; it is a set of connected ideas that need to be understood. When students understand the big ideas in mathematics, the methods and rules fall into place. One of the reasons any set of curriculum standards is flawed is that standards take the beautiful subject of mathematics and its many connections, and divide it into small pieces that make the connections disappear. Instead of starting with the small pieces, we have started with the big ideas and important connections, and have listed the relevant Common Core curriculum standards within the activities. Our activities invite students to engage in the mathematical acts that are listed in the imperative Common Core practice standards, and they also teach many of the Common Core content standards, which emerge from the rich activities. Student activity pages are noted with a ⊙ and teacher activity pages are noted with a ⊖.

Although we have chapters for each big idea, as though they are separate from each other, they are all intrinsically linked. Figure I.4 shows some of the connections between the ideas, and you may be able to see others. It is very important to share with students that mathematics is a subject of connections and to highlight the connections as students work. You may want to print the color visual of the different connections for students to see as they work. To see the maps of big ideas for all of the grades K through 8, find our paper "What Is Mathematical Beauty?" at youcubed.org.

Structure of the Book

Visualize. Play. Investigate. These three words provide the structure for each book in the series. They also pave the way for open student thinking, for powerful brain connections, for engagement, and for deep understanding. How do they do that? And why is this book so different from other mathematics curriculum books?

Visualize 🌀

For the past few years, I have been working with a neuroscience group at Stanford, under the direction of Vinod Menon, which specializes in mathematics learning. We have been working together to think about the ways that findings from brain science can be used to help learners of mathematics. One of the exciting discoveries that has

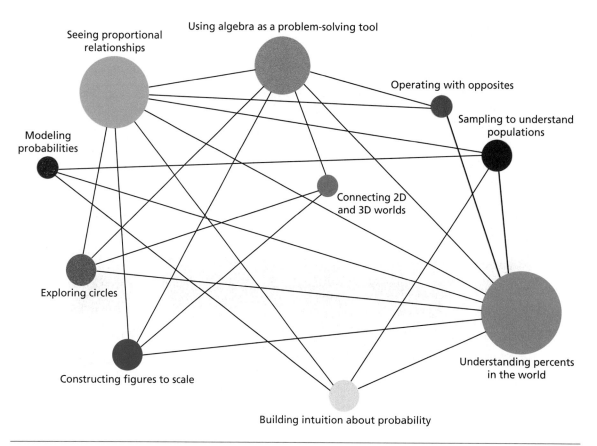

Seeing proportional relationships

Using algebra as a problem-solving tool

Operating with opposites

Sampling to understand populations

Modeling probabilities

Connecting 2D and 3D worlds

Exploring circles

Understanding percents in the world

Constructing figures to scale

Building intuition about probability

Figure I.4

been emerging over the last few years is the importance of visualizing for the brain and our learning of mathematics. Brain scientists now know that when we work on mathematics, even when we perform a bare number calculation, five areas of the brain are involved, as shown in Figure I.5.

Two of the five brain pathways—the dorsal and ventral pathways—are visual. The dorsal visual pathway is the main brain region for representing quantity. This may seem surprising, as so many of us have sat through hundreds of hours of mathematics classes working with numbers, while barely ever engaging visually with mathematics. Now brain scientists know that our brains "see" fingers when we calculate, and knowing fingers well—what they call finger perception—is critical for the development of an understanding of number. If you would like to read more about the importance of finger work in mathematics, look at the visual mathematics section of youcubed.org. Number lines are really helpful, as they provide the brain with a visual representation of number order. In one study, a mere four 15-minute sessions of students playing with a number line completely eradicated the differences between students from low-income and middle-income backgrounds coming into school (Siegler & Ramani, 2008).

Our brain wants to think visually about mathematics, yet few curriculum materials engage students in visual thinking. Some mathematics books show

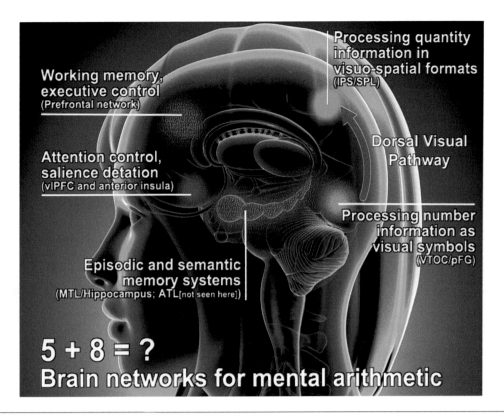

Working memory, executive control (Prefrontal network)

Attention control, salience detation (vlPFC and anterior insula)

Episodic and semantic memory systems (MTL/Hippocampus; ATL[not seen here])

Processing quantity information in visuo-spatial formats (IPS/SPL)

Dorsal Visual Pathway

Processing number information as visual symbols (VTOC/pFG)

5 + 8 = ?
Brain networks for mental arithmetic

Figure I.5

pictures, but they rarely ever invite students to do their own visualizing and drawing. The neuroscientists' research shows the importance not only of visual thinking but also of students' connecting different areas of their brains as they work on mathematics. The scientists now know that as children learn and develop, they increase the connections between different parts of the brain, and they particularly develop connections between symbolic and visual representations of numbers. Increased mathematics achievement comes about when students are developing those connections. For so long, our emphasis in mathematics education has been on symbolic representations of numbers, with students developing one area of the brain that is concerned with symbolic number representation. A more productive and engaging approach is to develop all areas of the brain that are involved in mathematical thinking, and visual connections are critical to this development.

In addition to the brain development that occurs when students think visually, we have found that visual activities are really engaging for students. Even students who think they are "not visual learners" (an incorrect idea) become fascinated and think deeply about mathematics that is shown visually—such as the visual representations of the calculation 18 × 5 shown in Figure I.6.

In our Youcubed teaching of summer school to sixth- and seventh-grade students and in our trialing of Youcubed's WIM materials, we have found

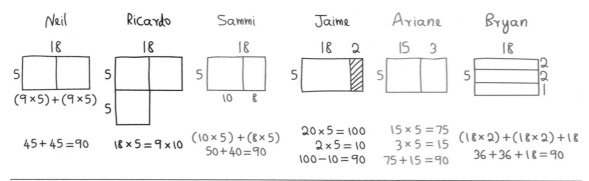

Figure I.6

that students are inspired by the creativity that is possible when mathematics is visual. When we were trialing the materials in a local middle school one day, a parent stopped me and asked what we had been doing. She said that her daughter had always said she hated and couldn't do math, but after working on our tasks, she came home saying she could see a future for herself in mathematics. We had been working on the number visuals that we use throughout these teaching materials, shown in Figure I.7.

The parent reported that when her daughter had seen the creativity possible in mathematics, everything had changed for her. I strongly believe that we can give these insights and inspirations to many more learners with the sort of creative, open mathematics tasks that fill this book.

We have also found that when we present visual activities to students, the status differences that often get in the way of good mathematics teaching disappear. I was visiting a first-grade classroom recently, and the teacher had set up four different stations around the room. In all of them, the students were working on arithmetic. In one, the teacher engaged students in a mini number talk; in another, a teaching assistant worked on an activity with coins; in the third, the students played a board game; and in the fourth, they worked on a number worksheet. In each of the first three stations, the students collaborated and worked really well, but as soon as students went to the worksheet station, conversations changed, and in every group I heard statements like "This is easy," "I've finished," "I can't do this," and "Haven't you finished yet?" These status comments are unfortunate and off-putting for many students. I now try to present mathematical tasks without numbers as often as possible, or I take out the calculation part of a task, as it is the numerical and calculational aspects that often cause students to feel less sure of themselves. This doesn't mean that students cannot have a wonderful and productive relationship with numbers, as we hope to promote in this book, but sometimes the key mathematical idea can be arrived at without any numbers at all.

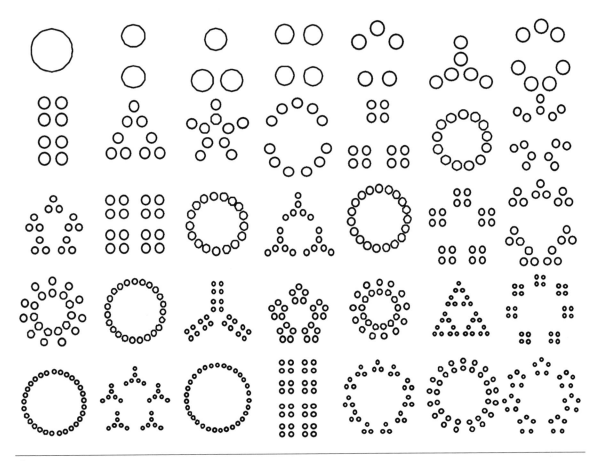

Figure I.7

Almost all the tasks in our book invite students to think visually about mathematics and to connect visual and numerical representations. This encourages important brain connections as well as deep student engagement.

Play 🧩

The key to reducing status differences in mathematics classrooms, in my view, comes from *opening* mathematics. When we teach students that we can see or approach any mathematical idea in different ways, they start to respect the different thinking of all students. Opening mathematics involves inviting students to see ideas differently, explore with ideas, and ask their own questions. Students can gain access to the same mathematical ideas and methods through creativity and exploration that they can by being taught methods that they practice. As well as reducing or removing status differences, open mathematics is more engaging for students. This is why we are inviting students, through these mathematics materials, to play with mathematics. Albert Einstein famously once said that "play is the highest form of research." This is because play is an opportunity for ideas to be used and developed in the service of something enjoyable. In the Play activities of our materials, students are invited to work with an important idea in a free space where they can enjoy the freedom of mathematical play. This does not mean that the activities do not teach essential mathematical content and practices—they do, as they invite students to work with the ideas. We have designed the Play activities to downplay competition and instead invite students to work with each other, building understanding together.

Investigate ❓

Our Investigate activities add something very important: they give students opportunities to take ideas to the sky. They also have a playful element, but the difference is that they pose questions that students can explore and take to very high levels. As I mentioned earlier, all of our tasks are designed to be as low floor and high ceiling as possible, as these provide the best conditions for engaging all students, whatever their prior knowledge. Any student can access them, and students can take the ideas to high levels. We should always be open to being surprised by what our learners can do, and always provide all students with opportunities to take work to high levels and to be challenged.

A crucial finding from neuroscience is the importance of students struggling and making mistakes—these are the times when brains grow the most. In one of my meetings with a leading neuroscientist, he stated it very clearly: if students are not struggling, they are not learning. We want to put students into situations where they feel that work is hard, but within their reach. Do not worry if students ask questions that you don't know the answer to; that is a good thing. One of the damaging ideas that teachers and students share in education is that teachers of mathematics know everything. This gives students the idea that mathematics people are those who know a lot and never make mistakes, which is an incorrect and harmful message. It is good to say to your students, "That is a great question that we can all think about" or "I have never thought about that idea; let's investigate it together." It is even good to make mistakes in front of students, as it shows them that mistakes are an important part of mathematical work. As they investigate, they should be going to places you have never thought about—taking ideas in new directions and exploring uncharted territory. Model for students what it means to be a curious mathematics learner, always open to learning new ideas and being challenged yourself.

* * *

We have designed activities to take at least a class period, but some of them could go longer, especially if students ask deep questions or start an investigation into a cool idea. If you can be flexible about students' time on activities, that is ideal, or you may wish to suggest that students continue activities at home. In our teaching of these activities, we have found that students are so excited by the ideas that they take them home to their families and continue working on them, which is wonderful. At all times, celebrate deep thinking over speed, as that is the nature of real mathematical thought. Ask students to come up with creative representations of their ideas; celebrate their drawing, modeling, and any form of creativity. Invite your students into a journey of mathematical curiosity and take that journey with them, walking by their side as they experience the wonder of open, mindset mathematics.

References

Lockhart, P. (2012). *Measurement*. Cambridge, MA: Harvard University Press.

Siegler, R. S., & Ramani, G. B. (2008). Playing linear numerical board games promotes low income children's numerical development. *Developmental Science, 11*(5), 655–661. doi:10.1111/j.1467-7687.2008.00714.x

Thurston, W. (1990). Mathematical education. *Notices of the American Mathematical Society, 37*(7), 844–850.

Note on Materials

In middle schools, we often find that there is little use of manipulatives and that few may be available in the building for teachers to choose from. But we believe, and extensive research supports, that all math learners benefit from mathematics that is visual, concrete, and modeled in multiple representations. Students need to physically create, draw, and construct mathematics to build deep understanding of what concepts represent and mean. Students need to interact with mathematics, manipulating representations to pose and investigate questions. Apps and digital games are another option, and we have found them to be valuable because they can be organized and manipulated with an unending supply. However, we want to emphasize that they should not be a replacement for the tactile experience of working with physical manipulatives. We support making different tools available for students to use as they see fit for the representation, and, following the activity, we encourage you to ask students to reflect on what the tools allowed them to see mathematically.

In our books for middle grades, you will find the same emphasis on visual mathematics and using manipulatives as in our elementary books, because these representations of mathematics are critical for all learners. If manipulatives are in short supply in your building, we encourage you to advocate for their purchase for the long-term benefit of your students. In the near term, you may be able to borrow the manipulatives we use in this book from your district's elementary schools.

Manipulatives and Materials Used in This Book

- **Snap cubes.** Snap or multilink cubes enable students to construct three-dimensional solids using cubic units. These are particularly useful in exploring volume and the connections between two- and three-dimensional space, but they can also be used for patterning, representing mathematical situations, and measurement.

- **Centimeter cubes.** Centimeter cubes are wonderful tools for exploring volume while being precise about that volume using conventional units of measure. In seventh grade, however, we've used these tools as small objects to toss in a probability game.

- **Square tiles.** Square tiles are a flexible manipulative that can be used to literally represent square units for conceptualizing area and covering surfaces. They can also be used to represent patterns visually that are too often only represented symbolically, making them a useful algebraic manipulative.

- **Geometric solids.** Geometric solids allow students to touch, rotate, and sometimes decompose three-dimensional figures of different types. Some solids can be filled to explore volume. We use these solids in this book to support students in building their own versions out of clay.

- **Dice.** Dice are used for game play and to explore probability. Here we reference typical six-sided dice, but we encourage you to explore the world of dice with different numbers of sides and values. Changing dice can change what ideas students have opportunities to explore.

- **Geoboards and rubber bands.** Geoboards allow students to create, revise, and test geometric figures on either a square or isometric grid. They can be used to investigate area, angles, slope, transformations, and properties of shapes. In seventh grade, we use them for a specific investigation of probability that requires large isometric geoboards, which can sometimes be found on the reverse of square geoboards. Students need a range of rubber band sizes to create shapes of different sizes across the entire geoboard.

- **Rulers.** We use rulers as linear measurement tools to explore the connections between dimensions of circles and to build conceptual understanding of pi. Rulers are also used throughout as straightedges in the construction of graphs.

- **Colors.** Color-coding work is a powerful tool to support decomposition, patterning, and connecting representations. We often ask that students have access to colors; whether they are markers, colored pencils, or colored pens, we leave up to you.

- **Adding machine tape.** Adding machine tape is an unsung hero of manipulatives. Students can create their own measurement tools, decompose linear spaces into units or fractions, construct number lines, fold and investigate symmetry, and connect all of these ideas together. Adding machine tape can be used to measure distances, particularly those with curves. Further, adding machine tape can be made any length, written on, diagrammed, and color-coded. It is so inexpensive that students can make lots of mistakes and feel safe.

- **Clay or kinetic sand and cutting tools.** Moldable material is an uncommon manipulative, but we think it is important for students investigating three-dimensional figures to be able to build and manipulate them. Clay is stiff and can withstand slicing with wire, dental floss, or plastic knives, though some of these tools work better with different kinds of clay. Kinetic sand is more expensive, but has the admirable quality of being easily moldable and releasing well while maintaining crisp edges.

- **Collections of small objects.** Collections of objects offer students of all ages the opportunity to interact with, count, estimate, and make inferences about the collection and its members. In most cases, there are many different types of objects that can support this kind of mathematical work, such as beads, coins, sequins, dried beans or grains, or buttons. In seventh grade, what matters is that these collections, or populations, have some variation (such as color, shape, or type) so that students can explore differences within the collection.

- **Paper towel rolls, toilet paper rolls, or cardboard tubes and foam.** As part of our investigation of circles, we invite students to explore the length of a roll of foam, which spirals to create a large cylinder. We suggest these materials for modeling this task to support this investigation. As with all mathematical activities, modeling the problem, particularly concretely, can offer entry points for all students to think about complex ideas.

- **Calculators.** Calculators are used as a resource in the book to allow students to focus on the bigger mathematical ideas, rather than spending their time performing calculations. Calculators are a tool that students need to know how to use, and they should increase students' access to big mathematical ideas.

- **Office supplies, such as paper clips, tape, glue sticks, and masking tape.** We use these across the book to construct charts, serve as markers in games or activities, mark spaces, display thinking, or piece together work.

Activities for Building Norms

Encouraging Good Group Work

We always use this activity before students work on math together, as it helps improve group interactions. Teachers who have tried this activity have been pleased by students' thoughtful responses and found the students' thoughts and words helpful in creating a positive and supportive environment. The first thing to do is to ask students, in groups, to reflect on things they don't like people to say or do in a group when they are working on math together. Students come up with quite a few important ideas, such as not liking people to give away the answer, to rush through the work, or to ignore other people's ideas. When students have had enough time in groups brainstorming, collect the ideas. We usually do this by making a What We Don't Like list or poster and asking each group to contribute one idea, moving around the room until a few good ideas have been shared (usually about 10). Then we do the same for the What We Do Like list or poster. It can be good to present the final posters to the class as the agreed-on classroom norms that you and they can reflect back on over the year. If any student shares a negative comment, such as "I don't like waiting for slow people," do not put it on the poster; instead use it as a chance to discuss the issue. This rarely happens, and students are usually very thoughtful and respectful in the ideas they share.

Activity	Time	Description/Prompt	Materials
Launch	5 min	Explain to students that working in groups is an important part of what mathematicians do. Mathematicians discuss their ideas and work together to solve challenging problems. It's important to work together, and we need to discuss what helps us work well together.	
Explore	10 min	Assign a group facilitator to make sure that all students get to share their thoughts on points 1 and 2. Groups should record every group member's ideas and then decide which they will share during the whole-class discussion. In your groups . . . 1. Reflect on the things you do not like people to say or do when you are working on math together in a group. 2. Reflect on the things you do like people to say or do when you are working on math together in a group.	• Paper • Pencil or pen
Discuss	10 min	Ask each group to share their findings. Condense their responses and make a poster so that the student ideas are visible and you can refer to them during the class.	Two to four pieces of large poster paper to collect the students' ideas

Paper Folding: Learning to Reason, Convince, and Be a Skeptic

Connection to CCSS
6.G.3
6.G.4

One of the most important topics in mathematics is reasoning. Whereas scientists prove or disprove ideas by finding cases, mathematicians prove their ideas by reasoning—making logical connections between ideas. This activity gives students an opportunity to learn to reason well by having to convince others who are being skeptical.

Before beginning the activity, explain to students that their role is to be convincing. The easiest person to convince is yourself. A higher level of being convincing is to convince a friend, and the highest level of all is to convince a skeptic. In this activity, the students learn to reason to the extent that they can convince a skeptic. Students should work in pairs and take turns to be the one convincing and the one being a skeptic.

Give each student a square piece of paper. If you already have 8.5 × 11 paper, you can ask them to make the square first.

The first challenge is for one of the students to fold the paper to make a scalene triangle that does not include any of the edges of the paper. They should convince their partner that it is a scalene triangle, using what she knows about scalene triangles to be convincing. The skeptic partner should ask lots of skeptical questions, such as "How do you know that the sides all have different lengths?" and not accept that they are because it looks like they are.

The partners should then switch roles, and the other student folds the paper into a rectangle, that does not include any of the edges of the paper. Their partner should be skeptical and push for high levels of reasoning.

The partners should then switch again, and the challenge is to fold the paper to make a rhombus, again not using the edges of the paper.

The fourth challenge is to make a rhombus that is not a square. The rhombus should be different than the one made in the third challenge. For each challenge, partners must reason and be skeptical.

When the task is complete, facilitate a whole-class discussion in which students discuss the following questions:

- Which was the most challenging task? Why?
- What was hard about reasoning and being convincing?
- What was hard about being a skeptic?

Activity	Time	Description/Prompt	Materials
Launch	5 min	Tell students that their role for the day is to be convincing and to be a skeptic. Ask students to fold a piece of paper into a square. Choose a student and model being a skeptic.	

Activity	Time	Description/Prompt	Materials
Explore	10 min	Show students the task and explain that in each round, they are to solve the folding problem. In pairs, students alternate folding and reasoning and being the skeptic. After students convince themselves they have solved each problem, they switch roles and fold the next challenge. Give students square paper or ask them to start by making a square. The convincing challenges are as follows: 1. Fold your paper into a scalene triangle that does not include any edges of the paper. 2. Fold your paper into a rectangle that does not include any edges of the paper. 3. Fold your paper into a rhombus that does not include any edges of the paper. 4. Fold your paper into a different rhombus that is not a square and does not include any edges of the paper.	• One piece of 8.5" × 11" paper per student • Paper Folding worksheet for each student
Discuss	10 min	Discuss the activity as a class. Make sure to discuss the roles of convincer and skeptic.	

Paper Folding: Learning to Reason, Convince, and Be a Skeptic

1. Fold your paper into a scalene triangle that does not include any edges of the paper. Convince a skeptic that it is a scalene triangle.
   Reflection:

   Switch roles

2. Fold your paper into a rectangle that does not include any edges of the paper. Convince a skeptic that it is a rectangle.
   Reflection:

   Switch roles

3. Fold your paper into a rhombus that does not include any edges of the paper. Convince a skeptic that it is a rhombus.
   Reflection:

   Switch roles

4. Fold your paper into a different rhombus that is not a square that does not include any edges of the paper. Convince a skeptic that it is a rhombus.
   Reflection:

BIG IDEA 1

Connecting 2D and 3D Worlds

Researchers have recently shown that when we work on a mathematics problem, five areas of the brain are involved, and two of them are visual pathways (Menon, 2015) (as I explained in the introduction to this book). Our brains are helped when we work visually; and when we connect visuals with numbers, important brain connections occur. In addition, other brain areas are involved when we touch, move things, and interact physically with mathematical ideas. The area of research concerning physical touch and movement is known as "embodied cognition," and researchers in this field point out the importance of students' holding mathematical ideas in the motor and perceptual areas of the brain (Nemirovsky, Rasmussen, Sweeney, & Wawro, 2012), which comes about when they learn mathematical ideas through touch and movement. In this big idea, students are learning about the features of 3D shapes. This is an area that is particularly important to experience physically, as students will not develop a complete understanding of the mathematical features of shapes if they only see them in two-dimensional pictures in textbooks.

When we taught 83 middle school students a few summers ago, we invited them to build larger cubes out of sugar cubes. A year later, one of the students told me that he still remembers the meaning of "1 cubed" by recalling the feel and the features of the small cube he held in his hands. He told me that it was continuing to help him as he learned geometry. The three activities in this big idea give students a physical opportunity to hold objects in their hands and experience their different features.

In the Visualize activity, students are invited to slice 3D objects to make different two-dimensional shapes. Students will enjoy working with clay, and they will learn about the three-dimensional objects they hold in their hands as they touch and feel the dimensions. As they form the shapes and then sketch them, they will be able to make connections between areas of the brain that deal with physical touch and with drawing.

In the Play activity, students will get the opportunity to explore further with the objects they build out of clay. This activity also includes an element we design into tasks wherever possible—giving students choice. This is something that will increase their interest, which, in turn, will increase their learning and achievement.

Our Investigate activity poses questions that we hope will enable students to struggle, as that causes positive brain activity, and to extend their ideas to high levels. The questions have an openness that is rare in textbooks but that is important, as this openness enables students to develop their own ideas and to develop mathematical thinking in response to ill-defined problems of the type they will meet in the world outside school. We pose the following questions:

- How could you slice this solid so that the face that is made has the same area as the base?
- How could you slice it so that the shape has an area bigger than the base?

Both questions will give students opportunities to think deeply, to wonder about relationships, and to connect ideas.

Jo Boaler

References

Menon, V. (2015). Salience network. In A. W. Toga (Ed.), *Brain mapping: An encyclopedic reference* (Vol. 2, pp. 597–611). San Diego, CA: Academic Press.

Nemirovsky, R., Rasmussen, C., Sweeney, G., & Wawro, M. (2012). When the classroom floor becomes the complex plane: Addition and multiplication as ways of bodily navigation. *Journal of the Learning Sciences, 21*(2), 287–323. doi:10.1080/10508406 .2011.611445

Seeing Slices

Snapshot

Students visualize and explore the two-dimensional shapes that can be made by slicing a rectangular solid.

Connection to CCSS
7.G.3

Agenda

Activity	Time	Description/ Prompt	Materials
Launch	10–15 min	Show students a rectangular solid made of clay, and then slice that solid on an angle. Without separating the pieces, ask student to predict what shape the face of the slice is. Discuss students' predictions, then reveal and discuss the shape of the face.	• Rectangular solid made of clay • Cutting tool (dental floss or a wire cutter)
Explore	25–30 min	Small groups explore the question, What different two-dimensional shapes can you make by slicing a rectangular prism? Groups create a rectangular solid from clay and a net to match. Then groups use a cutting tool to slice and re-form the solid repeatedly to explore the shapes of the sliced faces. Students sketch the solid, how it was sliced, and the resulting face shape.	• Clay, enough for each group to form a rectangular solid • Cutting tool (dental floss or a wire cutter), for each group • Regular and isometric dot paper (see appendix), multiple sheets per group
Discuss	15 min	Discuss the two-dimensional shapes students created by slicing their rectangular solids. Discuss patterns for creating rectangles, other quadrilaterals, or triangles. Ask, What shapes cannot be made? Why?	Optional: chart and markers

To the Teacher

For this activity and the others in this big idea, we want students to have the chance to physically interact with three-dimensional figures and have the opportunity to slice them. To accomplish this, we recommend the use of clay to make the solids and dental floss for cutting. If you have an art department that has wire cutters for clay, those are even better. You may also try plastic knives, if you have those available. We like clay because it is stiff, and if you use a thin cutting tool, clay will maintain the shape of the slice better than play dough or other softer modeling substances. We recommend that you try working with the clay yourself to see what strategies work best with your specific clay for forming crisp solids and slicing them so that the solid does not warp. This will make it easier for you to model your cutting technique for the class during the launch. You may want to provide tips to the class for forming solids and cutting smoothly based on your experience. One additional option instead of clay is kinetic sand. It is much more expensive, which is why we have not focused on it here, but it molds beautifully, with crisp edges, and cuts well.

Students may notice that slicing a prism makes two different kinds of shapes: two new three-dimensional solids and a new two-dimensional face. In this activity, we're going to focus on the two-dimensional face made by slicing. However, you'll want to be precise with your language to avoid confusion. For instance, if you simply asked, What shape is made by slicing the rectangular solid? students may try to name the new *solids* created, rather than the shape of the new *face* created.

In the closing discussion, we ask the class to consider patterns for slicing the rectangular solid to get different kinds of face shapes. An exhaustive list is not necessary, but we hope that students will discover that to create a rectangle, they can slice parallel or perpendicular to one of the rectangular faces. To make a triangular slice, you must slice through only three faces, which looks like slicing a corner off the solid. Encourage students to look for as many patterns as they can.

A vertical cut perpendicular to the base.

A diagonal slice passing through three faces.

The shape of the cut through three faces is a triangle.

Activity

Launch

Launch the activity by showing students a rectangular prism made out of clay. Your rectangular prism should be large enough that students can see it well, and the faces, edges, and vertices should be as crisp as possible. Show students your cutting tool (dental floss or wire cutter), and then use it to cut the clay into two parts on an angle, so that your cut is not parallel to one face.

The square prism sliced diagonally.

Without separating the two pieces, ask the class, What shape do you think the face of the slice is? Give students a chance to turn and talk to a partner about how they are visualizing the face made by slicing the solid. Invite students to come up and draw their hypotheses on the board or document camera. Ask students to explain why they believe that their shape is the one made by the slice. For each predication, ask the class whether they agree or disagree and why. The class may not come to agreement on a prediction, but do invest some time in debating predictions and how students are visualizing the slice.

Separate the two pieces of the rectangular solid to reveal the shape of the sliced face. Trace the shape of the slice onto a piece of paper on the document camera or onto the board. Discuss what you found and its relationship with students' ideas. Ask, How accurate were our predictions? Does the shape surprise you? Why or why not?

Pose the question for exploration: What different two-dimensional shapes can you make by slicing a rectangular prism?

Explore

Provide each group with clay, a cutting tool, and isometric and regular dot paper (see appendix). Ask each group to make a rectangular prism and construct a net for that prism on the regular dot paper as a record of their solid. Students explore the question, What different two-dimensional shapes can you make by slicing a rectangular prism?

Students cut the solid they have formed so as to find different shapes that can be made by slicing. For each slice, the group makes a sketch of how they cut the solid and traces the sliced face to record the new shape created. Students may find that isometric dot paper is useful for sketching the solid and their cut lines, while the regular dot paper is more useful for tracing the shape of the sliced face. Students can use their net to help them re-form the same solid as they cut it again and again.

Discuss

Ask, What shapes were you able to make by slicing your rectangular prisms? Invite groups to share some examples of how they cut and the shapes they made.

Discuss the following questions:

- How do you cut the rectangular prism to get different sorts of shapes?
- What are the rules for cutting to get a rectangle? Or a quadrilateral? Or a triangle? (For each kind of shape students created, discuss the ways they must slice to produce that shape. You may want to record these patterns on a chart.)
- What shapes are not possible when slicing a rectangular solid? Why?

Look-Fors

- **Are students interpreting the shape of the face accurately?** As described in the To the Teacher section, students may struggle to interpret which shape they are exploring—the two new solids created by slicing, the new two-dimensional face made by slicing, or even the changed two-dimensional faces of the former rectangular solid. In the launch, we encourage you to be as clear as possible, but if you see students interpreting the task differently, you may want to get your rectangular solid model and point out the feature under investigation. Further, even if students understand that it is the face we are thinking closely about, their eyes may play tricks on them. Students may observe a cut face that is a quadrilateral and see it as a rectangle or parallelogram, even when it is not. Ask probing questions such as, How do you know it is a rectangle (or parallelogram)? How can we be sure? What happens when you trace it onto the dot paper? Be sure students are using more than their eyes to name the shapes they create.

- **How are students sketching their solids?** Making two-dimensional representations of three-dimensional solids is challenging, because it can be difficult for the eye to translate what it sees in the three-dimensional space onto a flat surface. Isometric dot paper (see appendix) can help students capture the depth of a shape, but even the use of this tool requires students to take something they understand and represent it somewhat differently than it is in the real world. For instance, students will know that the faces of their solid are rectangular, but to draw the solid with depth, students will need to represent some faces as parallelograms. If students are struggling with the difference between what they know about a shape and how to draw it, encourage them to look closely at the solid from one angle and describe what the faces *look* like from that angle—not what they actually *are*, but what they look like. Students may need to first challenge what they *see* to be able to draw it.

- **Are students noticing patterns?** Students may focus on cutting, sketching, and re-forming their solids, but looking for patterns is a goal of this exploration. As you circulate to talk to groups, deliberately ask students, What patterns are you noticing in the shapes you can make by slicing your solid? Students may not have thought about patterns yet, but your question will prompt them to reflect on the many shapes they have created to look for patterns. Note also whether students seem to be cutting repeatedly, but in the same ways, which will constrain what patterns they can see and what shapes they find. If you notice that they are, for instance, always cutting parallel to one face of the solid, you might ask, What happens if you cut on an angle?

Reflect

When might you need to slice a solid? Why might the shape of the sliced face matter?

Playing with Clay

Snapshot

Students play with slicing a variety of three-dimensional figures to see what shapes the sliced faces can make and how these compare with slicing rectangular solids.

Connection to CCSS
7.G.3

Agenda

Activity	Time	Description/ Prompt	Materials
Launch	5 min	Remind students of the two-dimensional shapes they made by slicing rectangular prisms. Show students some of the figures in the solid set. Ask, If we sliced a different solid, how might that change the shapes the slice could make?	Solid set
Explore	20 min	Each group selects a solid to explore, and forms one like it using clay. Groups construct a net for their solid as a record. Students form hypotheses about the two-dimensional shapes that could be made by slicing the solid in different ways, and record their predictions.	• Slice Hypotheses sheet, one per group • Clay, for each group • Isometric and regular dot paper (see appendix), for each group • Solids, one per group
Discuss	10 min	Discuss the groups' hypotheses about the shapes that could be made by slicing their solids. Support students in describing how they visualized the slicing to make their predictions.	

Activity	Time	Description/ Prompt	Materials
Play	30+ min	Groups test their hypotheses by slicing their solid with a cutting tool repeatedly. For each slice, students record a sketch of how they sliced the figure and the new two-dimensional shape formed by the slice. Groups construct a chart for their solid that shows their hypotheses and their findings, using drawings and diagrams to make it as visual as possible.	• Slice Hypotheses sheet, one per group • Clay and a cutting tool, for each group • Isometric and regular dot paper (see appendix), for each group • Solids, one per group • Chart, markers, and tape, for each group
Discuss	15–20 min	Post groups' charts and do a brief gallery walk to look for patterns and surprises. Discuss what students found by slicing, how these findings compare to their hypotheses, and the patterns they notice looking across the different solids represented on charts. Discuss what shapes were not made and whether they might still be possible or are impossible.	

To the Teacher

In this activity, we continue to use clay and cutting tools to form and slice solids. See the To the Teacher section in the Visualize activity for more details about these materials. In addition to these, this activity requires a set of solids. You need only one set to make this activity work, as each group will explore only one figure. There are many types of solid sets available, ranging from those that are truly solid and made of wood to hollow figures that can be filled with water or sand, and even some with removable inserts that can unfold into nets. Any kind will work for this activity. However, if you do have available hollow solids, students may be able to use them as molds, making this activity more efficient. This is particularly effective if instead of clay you use kinetic sand, which molds easily and forms crisp edges.

Activity

Launch

Launch the activity by reminding students of the slicing work they did in the Visualize activity and the kinds of two-dimensional shapes they made by slicing rectangular prisms. Show students several three-dimensional figures from your solid set, such as cylinders, different kinds of prisms, pyramids, and spheres. Pose the question, If we sliced a different solid, how might that change the shapes the slice could make?

Explore

Provide each group with clay, isometric and regular dot paper (see appendix), and a Slice Hypotheses sheet. Invite each group to choose one solid from the solid set to explore. Ask each group to use the figure they chose to help them make a solid like it with clay. Groups then construct a net for that solid as a record, using regular dot paper.

Before students begin to play with slicing their solids, ask them to make a prediction, a formal hypothesis, of the shapes that could be made by slicing the solid. Encourage students to visualize different kinds of slices and sketch multiple predictions on the Slice Hypotheses sheet.

Discuss

Discuss the following questions:

- What are your hypotheses? What slice shapes might be made with your solid?
- How did you make your hypotheses? What were you seeing in your mind to help you predict the shape that would be formed by slicing?

Invite students to share their sketches or to hold up their solids to gesture the ways they imagine slicing it and what the results might be. Focus students' discussion on trying to visualize what is produced by slicing in different ways.

Play

Groups explore the question, What two-dimensional shapes can be made by slicing our solid? Provide each group with a cutting tool and invite them to cut the solid to find the different shapes that the sliced face can make. For each slice, students sketch on isometric dot paper a picture of how they cut the solid and trace the face (on isometric or regular dot paper) to record the slice shape. Students can use their net to help them re-form the solid and cut again.

Provide each group with chart, markers, and tape, and ask them to construct a display with their shape, their Slice Hypotheses sheet, and all the shapes they were able to make by slicing. Encourage students to make these displays as visual as possible to help others see the slicing they were trying.

Discuss

Have groups post their charts and do a short gallery walk. As students walk, ask them to look for patterns or surprises. Then gather the class to discuss the following questions:

- What shapes were you able to make by slicing your solids? How were they different than the shapes we made when slicing the rectangular solid? Invite students to share some examples of how they cut and the shapes they made.
- What patterns do you notice in the shapes of the slices that different groups made with different solids?
- What shapes were not possible with different solids? Why?
- Compare your hypotheses to what you found. How were they different? The same? Did you discover anything that surprised you?

Look-Fors

- **Are students making precise solids?** It can be physically difficult to work with clay and create solids with crisp edges and flat faces. However, the more precise the solid, the better the conclusions students can draw from slicing it. Although you don't want students spending inordinate amounts of time forming a meticulous solid, it makes sense to point out moments when greater precision will ultimately help students explore. You may want to notice aloud how the solid the group has created differs from the example from the solid set, or call attention to the challenges students face in trying to draw a net of a wobbly solid. Students may be supported with some tools with straight edges or flat faces to help them, such as rulers and the table top.
- **How are students dealing with ambiguity when slicing?** When students slice their solid, it is likely to warp somewhat. This makes exploring the shape of the sliced face a challenge. Ask students how they are dealing with the bends or crushed corners after they slice. Some students may discover that

they can reshape the face to re-create it. Ask, How do you know that this face is the shape of the slice, and not changed? What can you do to increase your confidence in your findings? As a test, students might try putting the two portions of the solid back together to see whether they meet accurately.

- **Are they slicing in new ways?** As in the Visualize activity, students may end up slicing the solid in similar ways repeatedly. This repeated slicing could be part of an important exploration of pattern. For instance, students exploring a pyramid might slice it parallel to the base repeatedly as they notice that they get similar figures of decreasing size as they move to the top vertex. However, this could also lead students to conclude that only a narrow set of slice shapes can be formed. Ask students questions about how they are deciding how to slice, the patterns they are noticing, and whether they can devise any creative slicing techniques to generate new shapes.

Reflect

What two-dimensional shapes have you not yet seen made by slicing? What kind of solid might you need to slice to get those shapes? How might you need to slice it?

 **Slice Hypotheses Sheet**

I think if we slice it like this . . .	It will make a slice like this . . .

The Area of Slices

Snapshot

Students investigate the area of faces made by slicing different types of geometric solids.

	Connection to CCSS
	7.G.3

Agenda

Activity	Time	Description/ Prompt	Materials
Launch	5–10 min	Remind students of their explorations of the shapes made by slicing solids. Pose the questions, How could you slice this solid so that the face that is made has the same area as the base? How could you slice it so that the shape has an area bigger than the area of the base?	Solid, either from solid set or made from clay
Explore	40+ min	Groups choose solids to explore, and develop conjectures about how to slice solids to yield shapes with the same area as the base, a larger area than the base, and the largest possible area. Students frame their conjectures as if-then statements and use grid paper to gather evidence about area.	• Make available: solid set • Clay and a cutting tool, for each group • Grid paper (see appendix), multiple sheets for each group
Discuss	20 min	Record students' conjectures on three charts, one for each question under investigation. Use the discussion to push students to be more precise about the conditions under which a conjecture might be true.	Charts and markers

Activity	Time	Description/ Prompt	Materials
Extend	20+ min	If the class is uncertain whether some conjectures are always true or true only under some conditions, send students back to construct new figures to test and refine these ideas. Discuss students' findings and revise your charts accordingly.	• Make available: solid set • Clay and a cutting tool, for each group • Grid paper (see appendix), multiple sheets for each group

To the Teacher

This activity builds on students' explorations of slicing solids in the previous two activities in this big idea. Here we incorporate area as an element of the investigation and invite students to make conjectures about how to slice solids to get an area that is the same as or larger than the base and then the largest possible area. Before students can grapple with this idea, the class must be clear about which faces of a solid can be called a *base*. For prisms, there are two faces that could be called the base; these are the two opposite faces joined by rectangles. For a triangular prism, these bases are triangles; for cylinders, they are the circles. For pyramids and cones, the base is opposite the vertex where the greatest number of faces meet. Spheres have no base. If students are unfamiliar with identifying bases, you'll want to include in your launch of the activity some discussion of what constitutes a base for these different sorts of figures.

When students begin to develop conjectures about the ways to slice three-dimensional figures to get the desired area, prisms are a nice entry point because they can lead to some more generalizable conjectures, rather than conjectures specific to each solid. For instance, when prisms are sliced parallel to the base, the slice is congruent to the base.

A pentagonal prism is sliced parallel to the base.

An octagonal prism is sliced parallel to the base.

A triangular prism is sliced parallel to the base.

When prisms are sliced at an angle (that is, not parallel to the base) and through the side faces, the area of the slice is larger than the area of the base. Students will have likely built some intuition about this in the Visualize and Play activities.

A square prism is sliced at an angle through five faces.

The shape of the cut face is traced.

The shape of the cut face is a pentagon.

These are fairly straightforward conjectures that can be supported by investigation of multiple solids. But it is important to note that these conjectures only apply to prisms, and if students extend their investigation to include pyramids and cones, they will find different patterns. Identifying the largest possible area of a slice is also trickier and depends more on the individual shape, if students push toward precision.

Activity

Launch

Launch this activity by reminding students of the work they have done visualizing the shapes made by slicing solids, and that they have found that many different shapes are possible no matter what the solid is. Tell students that today they are going to investigate not just the shapes that can be made but the size of these slices.

Hold up a solid from your solid set, or a clay solid you have made. Pose the questions, How could you slice this solid so that the face that is made has the same area as the base? How could you slice it so that the shape has an area bigger than the base? How do you slice the solid for the greatest possible area of the slice? Give students a chance to turn and talk to begin to think about these questions and visualize slicing the solids. Be sure the class is clear about which face(s) in different types of solids are considered the base.

Explore

Provide groups with clay, a cutting tool, regular or isometric dot paper (see appendix), and grid paper (see appendix). Invite students to choose a solid from the class's geometric solid set to make for this investigation. They can make more than one kind of three-dimensional figure as they try to develop conjectures to address the following questions:

- How would you slice a solid so that the slice has the same area as one of its bases?
- How would you slice a solid so that the slice has a bigger area than the base?
- How would you slice a solid for the greatest area possible?

Encourage student to frame their conjectures in the form of "If . . ., then . . ." For instance: "If you slice a prism parallel to its base, then the slice is the same shape and area as the base."

Students will need to check the area of the slices they make, using grid paper (see appendix). The areas that students find will likely not be precise because of the movement of the clay, but the results should provide students with enough evidence to make conjectures.

Discuss

Set up three posters for students' conjectures: "How to make a slice with the same area as a base," "How to make a slice with an area larger than a base," and "How to make a slice with the largest possible area." Set up each as a T-chart, with If . . . and Then . . . headers.

Student conjectures written as if . . . then . . . statements.

Moving poster by poster, collect students' conjectures and ask the class whether they have evidence that the conjecture is always true, sometimes true, or not true.

Highlight any conjectures about which the class seems unsure. Push students to defend the conditions under which a conjecture might be true. For instance, a conjecture that might be true for all prisms may not be true for any pyramid. As the discussion enables students to become more precise about these conditions, modify the If . . . column to show when a conjecture is true. Use the discussion to come to agreement about students' conjectures.

Extend

You can send the class back to make additional solids to test any conjectures about which the class was unsure of the conditions where it might hold true. Reconvene to discuss these conjectures and what students found.

Look-Fors

- **How are students using the grid paper to find the area of sliced faces?** The shapes of the sliced faces are likely to be somewhat imprecise, and finding area will involve some strategy. Students may count the squares on the grid paper, but they will need to deal with the partial squares to estimate the total area of the face. Partial units pose a challenge because when sides cut across multiple squares, students will need a method for approximating how these pieces can be assembled into whole units. Students can be more precise if they make the edges of the face neater and place the face on grid paper intentionally so that at least one edge aligns with the grid. If students become frustrated trying to estimate area, you'll want to zero in on which issue is at the root of their struggle—the shape of the face and its position on the paper, or developing methods for counting partial squares. Ask questions such as, What makes estimating the area hard? What could you try to make this easier?

- **Are students testing their ideas across shapes to generalize?** As students test individual slices on specific three-dimensional figures, they will generate several findings about these cases. Encourage students to think beyond these case-by-case findings and consider what the findings might indicate about general conclusions. You might ask, What patterns are you noticing about slicing and area? When do you seem to get an area the same as the base? When do you seem to get an area larger than the base? Stepping into generalizations can be a difficult move because students need to use the evidence they have to infer what would happen in cases they haven't yet tried. You might support students by asking them to think about what the pattern *might* be, and then asking how they could test this pattern to see whether it holds true.

- **How are students thinking about conditions for their conjectures?** On the other end of the generalization spectrum, students may be inclined to see a small amount of evidence and make sweeping generalizations about how to slice all solids. Ask students questions to encourage them to think about the conditions under which their conjectures hold and when they might not. You might ask, Will this work for all solids? Are there any solids where this pattern might not hold true? You might encourage students to go look at the solid set with one of their conjectures in mind and try to visualize whether it will work across all shapes. Students may also need support in developing more precise language about their conditions. For instance, students may need to use language such as *parallel, perpendicular, edges, faces,* and *vertices* in addition to the names of all the solids to help them name precisely how to slice those solids to yield the results they want.

Reflect

What other questions do you have about slicing solids? How might you investigate them?

Constructing Figures to Scale

This big idea is all about scaling measurements—or comparing one measurement to another. Whether they are scaling a length, an area, or a volume of something, students will need to think carefully about relationships. For when we increase a line by a scale, such as × 3, the length of the line is multiplied by 3. But when we scale the area of a shape, the area of the new shape is squared. This makes sense when we think about what is happening. For example, if I have a square of side 2, its area is 4.

If I double the side length, it becomes a 4 × 4 square, and its area becomes 16.

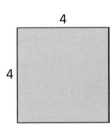

So by applying a scale factor of 2, we have doubled the side lengths (they are now 4), but we have squared the area. Not surprisingly, the impact of applying a scale factor to a volume is that the volume becomes cubed. Let's consider that. This time let's take our 2 × 2 square and apply a scale factor of 3.

Area of 4

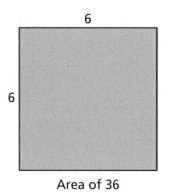

6

6

Area of 36

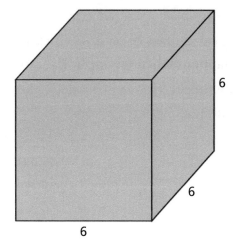

6

6

6

6

Volume is 6 × 6 × 6, which is 216.

If we look at these relationships, we see these patterns. A side of length 2 with a scale factor of 3 becomes a side of 6. The area (2 × 3) is squared, and the volume (2 × 3) is cubed. These relationships are ones that should, ideally, be discovered by students, so that they can think really carefully about them. Eleanor Duckworth is a Harvard educator who wrote an article titled "The Having of Wonderful Ideas." In this landmark publication, she recalls the children she had worked with who were allowed to discover mathematical relationships, and the ways that these were "transformational" moments for them. She says that she could have told them about the relationships, but it was the act of the students' finding them for themselves that made the mathematics so meaningful for them. In this set of activities, we give students opportunities to use scale factors and observe the impact of them when they apply them to lines, areas, and volumes.

In the Visualize activity, students are asked to consider the size of animals. At first they do not use the formal ideas of scale; instead they use intuition to think about size increases. The different animal examples have been chosen to pique students' interest about scale and its use in the world. Students will spend some time discussing the ideas of scale before learning about the ways scale can be used to give accurate information.

In the Play activity, students are invited to use data to correct a collection of fish drawings whose sizes are not shown accurately. The students are asked to use scale to work out the size of the fish accurately, and they are asked what they notice about what changes in the diagrams. This question leads to the Investigate activity, when students will be exploring the impact of scale on lines, areas, and volumes. Instead of telling students what happens when we apply scale to areas or volumes, we invite them to investigate these ideas and come up with their own conclusions about the relationships they discover. This time of investigation will help the students understand the relationships fully and remember them as they continue on their mathematical journeys.

Jo Boaler

Reference

Duckworth, E. (2006). "*The having of wonderful ideas" and other essays on teaching and learning*. New York, NY: Teachers College Press.

What Is Scale?

Snapshot

Students build on their intuition about scale to explore the measurement information embedded in scale images of animals and define the concept of scale.

	Connection to CCSS
	7.G.1, 7.RP.1

Agenda

Activity	Time	Description/Prompt	Materials
Launch	10 min	Show students the Forest Animals sheet and ask them to make observations. Tell them a bit about the Valdivian temperate rainforest to spark interest. Ask students how they might use the image to make inferences about the sizes of the animals.	Forest Animals sheet, to display
Explore	30 min	Partners use the information in the images to infer the sizes of the different animals shown. Students annotate their sheet to indicate relationships and how they found their measurements. Partners add one or more drawings to the sheet so that the drawings are represented in relationship to the other images shown.	• Forest Animals sheet, one per partnership • Colors, for each partnership • Make available: rulers or other measurement tools
Discuss	15–20 min	Partners share their inferences about size and use their observations to create a class-annotated image. Name that these inferences are possible because the images are *to scale*. Partners share the images they added and discuss how they did this so that relationships were accurate.	Forest Animals sheet, to display

To the Teacher

This activity focuses on building on students' intuition about scale before they use the concept with precision to calculate rates or similarity. Images provide an entry point for students to explore scale visually; images in books are typically meant to show something large reduced to fit on the page with scale in mind. Here we use scale to explore animals that are unexpected sizes.

We invite students to consider animal images shown to scale from two different ecosystems: North American temperate forests and the Valdivian temperate rain forest of Chile and Argentina. The North American woodland animals are likely familiar to many students, but have counterparts in the Valdivian rainforest that are surprisingly small. The Valdivian temperate rain forest has a climate similar to the Pacific Northwest and is a biodiversity hotspot. Many of the animals that live in this habitat live no other place and are under threat or endangered, including some of those shown on our sheet. However, the feature of these creatures that students are likely to find particularly compelling is their size: the pudu is the world's smallest deer, and the kodkod is the world's smallest cat. Allow students to use the scale images to discover the sizes of these animals; you may want to share details about these record-breaking animals in the closing discussion. We encourage you to learn a little about this unique habitat to share with your class when launching the activity.

Activity

Launch

Launch the activity by showing students the Forest Animals sheet on the document camera. Ask students, What do you notice about these images? What does the sheet show? Give students a chance to turn and talk, then invite students to share their observations. Be sure students notice that each animal is labeled with its name and that one reference length is provided.

Tell students a little bit about the Valdivian temperate rain forest to spark their interest. This is a region with animals related to those we know, but they are a very different size than the animals we're familiar with. Ask, How can we use this image to make inferences about the sizes of these animals? Give students a chance to turn and talk to generate some thinking.

Explore

Provide partners with a copy of the Forest Animals sheet and colors, and make rulers or other measurement tools available. Ask students to explore the question, How can we use this image to make inferences about the sizes of these animals?

Ask students to annotate the image with their inferences about the sizes of the animals shown. Encourage students to draw arrows or lines connecting animals to show their relationships or how they used one measurement to infer another.

Once partners have noted as many inferences as they can, invite them to add themselves, an animal of their own choosing, or an object to the image so that it is shown in relationship to the other images on the page. Ask, What can we learn about you, your animal, or the object from the drawing you made?

Discuss

Gather the class and put the Forest Animals sheet on the document camera. Ask partners to share the relationships they noticed and the inferences they made. Use their observations to make a class-annotated image. Collect as many inferences as you can.

Name for students that the reason we can make these inferences is that this is what is called a *scale* drawing, or we say that the image is *to scale*. This means that all of the images are shown in relationship to one another in the same way they are in life. Use some examples of students' thinking to show how they have already been using scale to make conclusions.

Invite students to share the images they've added. Ask students:

- How did you decide how to draw these images?
- How were you using the idea of scale here?
- What can we learn from the image this group added?

Look-Fors

- **Are students seeing relationships between images?** Students may treat each image as an individual source of information. If so, they will not be able to use the measurement data they already have to infer the length or height of other animals. You might challenge students by asking questions such as, What does the size of this animal tell us about the size of this other animal? How do you know? You might even need to directly tell students that these images are shown in relationship to each other. Ask, How can you use these relationships to figure out how long or tall these animals are?

- **How are students using precision?** The goal of this activity is not to prompt students to use proportions to calculate a precise length or height of the animals, but precision as a practice plays a role in building intuition about scale. Notice how students are making approximations. Are they using their fingers to measure lengths, or are they using rulers or other tools to be more precise? What degree of precision are students holding themselves to? For instance, rather than saying that two animals are about the same, are they measuring to find that one is a little longer than the other and reflecting those differences in their estimates?

- **What information are students using to construct their drawings?** As students move to adding an image, pay attention to the information students are using to construct these drawings. Do students make measurements, look up information in resources, or make estimates only? How are students using their inferred lengths and heights to approximate the drawings they construct? For instance, students could use the length of the deer to figure out how to draw a table, or they might find that they are five times the height of a pudu. These references should influence how they construct their drawings and be discussed at the end of the activity.

Reflect

What is scale?

Forest Animals

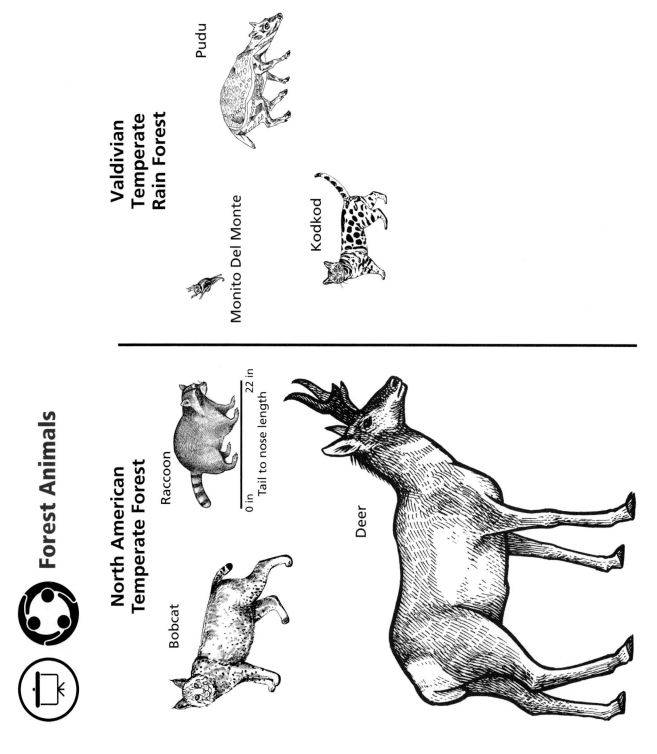

Valdivian Temperate Rain Forest

Pudu

Monito Del Monte

Kodkod

North American Temperate Forest

Raccoon

0 in — 22 in
Tail to nose length

Bobcat

Deer

Mindset Mathematics, Grade 7, copyright © 2019 by Jo Boaler, Jen Munson, Cathy Williams.
Reproduced by permission of John Wiley & Sons, Inc. *Sources:* shutterstock_328306349, shutterstock_618468692, shutterstock_723718432, shutterstock_773327740

A Fishy Image

Snapshot

Students play with scale by trying to use data to correct a collection of fish drawings that are not shown accurately in relationship to one another.

Connection to CCSS
7.G.1, 7.RP.2a,b, 7.RP.1

Agenda

Activity	Time	Description/Prompt	Materials
Launch	10 min	Show students A Fishy Image and the Fish Data sheet. Tell them that this image is not drawn to scale; the sizes of the fish are not shown accurately in relationship to one another. Tell students that their task is to find ways to fix this faulty image using the data they have.	• A Fishy Image, to display • Fish Data sheet, either to display or copied one per partnership
Play	30–45 min	Groups develop methods for finding errors in the scale drawings and creating their own image that represents all the fish in accurate relationship to one another.	• A Fishy Image and Fish Data sheet, one each per group • Make available: blank paper, colors, rulers, tape, dot paper, and grid paper (see appendix) • Chart and markers, for each group

Activity	Time	Description/Prompt	Materials
Discuss	15–20 min	Post groups' charts of their new images and do a gallery walk. Discuss the methods students developed to draw the fish to scale, why the images look different, and any disagreement about the accuracy of these new images.	

To the Teacher

In this activity, we move beyond an intuitive sense of scale to connecting scale to rates, which can be calculated with increased accuracy. We have provided an image and a data set that are problematic and provide students with the opportunity to develop rates for scale that can be used to check the flawed drawings and then to create their own images that better reflect proportional relationships. Students will be challenged by the choices involved; there are many different images they could create that would more accurately represent the measurement relationships between the fish. Each group will likely create a set of drawings at a different scale. Comparing these sets will reveal that they can all be correct within the set while also being different across the sets. Support students in thinking about why their solutions can be both different and correct while the original is different and incorrect. It all comes back to using a consistent scale within each set of illustrations.

Activity

Launch

Launch the activity by showing students A Fishy Image and the Fish Data sheet on the document camera. If you cannot display both simultaneously, you may want to copy the Fish Data sheet to hand out to partners as a reference as they look at A Fishy Image. You may want to invite students to study the data and image and see what they notice. Tell students that unlike the Forest Animals image, these animals are not drawn to scale. Each individual fish is accurate, but they are not shown accurately in relationship to one another. For instance, from this image you might think that a trout and a salmon are the same size, but they aren't. We can tell from the data table that the trout is an average of 16 inches and the salmon averages 28 inches.

Tell students that their task today is to fix this faulty image in whatever way they want. Be clear that this is not about artistic representation but rather about scale.

Play

Provide each group with copies of A Fishy Image and the Fish Data sheet, along with blank paper, rulers, colors, tape, dot paper (see appendix), and grid paper (see appendix). In small groups, students create a new image that shows the fish to scale. They work to develop methods for creating a set of scale images based on these fish and the data provided.

Students can represent the fish through sketches, diagrams, or even simple rectangles to show their size without drawing the details; this is not an artistic task, and students should be assured that their ability to reproduce the details of the fish is not the focus of this activity. Fish images can be on the same paper or on individual pieces of paper. Each image should be labeled so that everyone can see the relationships between the different types of fish.

Each group creates a poster that displays their new images and their process for fixing the original image, so that other groups will be convinced that their new images are to scale.

Discuss

Post groups' charts around the room and do a gallery walk. As students look at other groups' images, ask them to consider, Do these look right? Why or why not?

Discuss the following questions:

- What did you notice as you looked at the different images groups created? (Discuss why the images may be different *and* correct.)
- Are there any that you question? Why? (Discuss any aspects of the images that students do not agree are now to scale.)
- What methods did you all develop for fixing this fish image and showing the animals to scale? Which methods seemed to work? Why?
- How do the new images change what you notice about the different types of fish?

Look-Fors

- **Are students using rates?** One big idea that students can use to support their work is rates. Students will need to decide on a scale for their image, and that scale has a rate in which some linear measurement on the page represents a different linear measurement in the world. Students can use reasoning to determine whether two fish are clearly out of proportion, but to construct fish so that they are proportional, students will need to determine a scale or rate. As you ask students questions about the methods they are trying, probe their thinking to see whether they can articulate what the rate or scale is that they are using, or how they are using rate or scale to check the relationships between fish.

- **Are students fixing the original image or starting over?** When students plan to make accurate images of the fish, they might choose to do so by selecting one fish from the original image to serve as their scale and then change all of the fish that are shown out of proportion to this fish. This would be a strategy of fixing the image. If students choose this strategy, ask how they selected the fish to serve as their scale. Did they consider the size of the other fish when making their choice? Will they be able to draw the other fish reasonably using this new scale? Students may alternatively decide to start over because then they can choose the scale independent from the images they have been offered. Starting over has the advantage that students can select a scale that makes drawing simpler, such as 1 mm to 1 inch. Ask how they chose their scale and what it will mean for drawing all of the fish.

- **How are students recording their methods?** With many fish to re-create and several pieces of data to navigate, students can easily lose track of some of their process for determining the new fish lengths. Students could end up creating an image just as flawed as the original. Ask students questions about how they are tracking their work for each fish so that they can be confident in their new drawings. How are they using labels and units to help keep all the data straight? Will others be able to follow their process or check their work if they are uncertain? What could they add to their work, or how could they organize it so that it makes it easier for others to understand?

Reflect

Why are scale drawings useful?

A Fishy Image

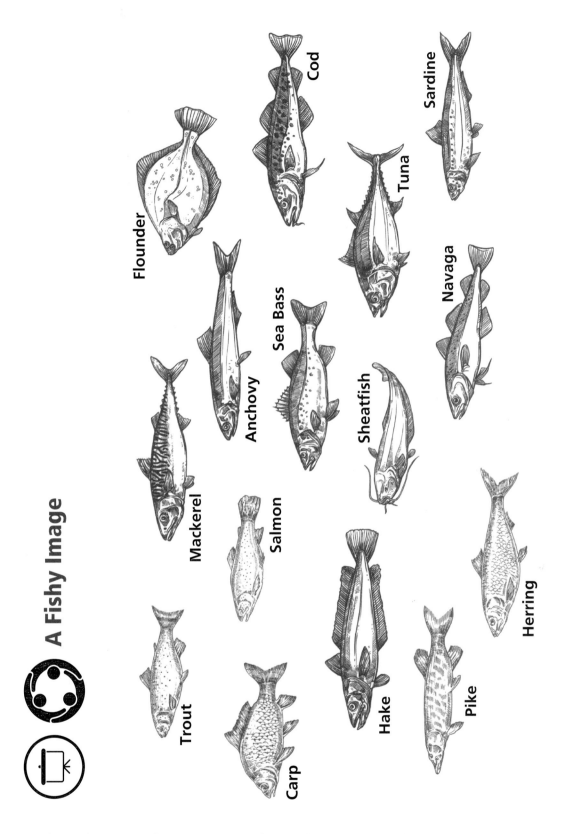

Type of Fish	Average Length (Inches)
Trout	16
Carp	23
Salmon	28
Pike	19
Mackerel	12
Hake	30
Herring	14
Sheatfish	108
Sea Bass	36
Tuna	156
Navaga	20
Anchovy	4
Cod	32
Sardine	7
Flounder	24

Magnifying Solids

Snapshot

When you scale up a solid, what happens to its surface area and volume? Students explore how scale is related across linear measurement, area, and volume for rectangular prisms.

Connection to CCSS
7.G.1, 7.G.6, 7.RP.2b,c

Agenda

Activity	Time	Description/Prompt	Materials
Launch	10 min	Show students two rectangular solids made from snap cubes, one that has side lengths double the other. Ask students how the solid has been doubled, and come to agreement that it was each of the side lengths that was doubled. Pose questions about the patterns in solids' surface areas and volumes that emerge when you double or triple the side lengths.	Two simple rectangular solids, one of which has side lengths double the other, constructed out of snap cubes
Explore	45+ min	Groups investigate what happens to the surface area and volume of a rectangular solid when they scale it up. Students construct their own series of solids, nets, and drawings to explore patterns. Groups organize their data and findings on a chart.	• Snap cubes, 100 or more per group • Chart and markers, for each group • Make available: grid paper, snap cube grid paper, isometric dot paper (see appendix for all three types), scissors, tape, and rulers

Activity	Time	Description/Prompt	Materials
Discuss	20 min	Post groups' charts and do a gallery walk. Discuss the patterns students found in surface area and volume as they scaled up their rectangular solid, and whether these patterns hold true regardless of the starting solid. Discuss ways of naming and noting these patterns with words, and possibly symbols, such as exponents.	
Extend	45+ min	Students investigate whether the same patterns in surface area and volume hold true when scaling up other kinds of prisms, such as triangular prisms or hexagonal prisms. Groups construct models by drawing on dot and grid paper and create a chart to display findings. Discuss why the patterns that students identified make sense.	• Chart and markers, for each group • Make available: grid paper, snap cube grid paper, isometric dot paper (see appendix for all three types), scissors, tape, and rulers

To the Teacher

This activity explores what happens to area (measured in square units) and volume (measured in cubic units) when the linear measurement of the side lengths are scaled up. Doubling the side lengths of a solid, such as the two shown in Figure 2.1, does not simply double all of the measured attributes of the figure. The surface area of a $2 \times 2 \times 1$ solid is 16 square units. But when you double the side lengths, the resulting $4 \times 4 \times 2$ solid has a surface area of 64 square units. The surface area does not double; it grows by 2^2, or quadruples. Volume has its own pattern. The $2 \times 2 \times 1$ solid has a volume of 4 cubic units, while the $4 \times 4 \times 2$ solid has a volume of 32 cubic units. The volume does not double; it grows by 2^3, or 8 times.

Figure 2.1 A 2 × 2 × 1 solid turns into a 4 × 4 × 2 solid when the side lengths are doubled. What happens to the size of the nets and the volume?

Knowing that these solids are going to grow exponentially, encourage students to start small. Invite them to construct a starter solid such as a 1 × 1 × 1, 2 × 2 × 1, or 3 × 2 × 2. Even when starting small, students will need access to a lot of snap cubes to be able to construct solids that scale up by a factor of 2, 3, 4, or beyond as they look for patterns.

You can use this investigation as an introduction to exponents, by using exponents as a notation for the patterns of growth students discover. While this notation is not needed to uncover or discuss these patterns, the activity is an excellent opportunity to name this pattern as exponential growth or to use exponents to label clearly their thinking.

Activity

Launch

Launch the activity by showing students a simple solid you have made out of snap cubes (such as 2 × 2 × 1) and another solid in which the side lengths are doubled (4 × 4 × 2 in this case). Display these solids so that students can clearly see how they are constructed and could count the side lengths if they wished. Tell students that you first made the smaller one and then decided to double it to make the larger one. Note that this is a deliberately vague statement.

Ask, What did I do to the original solid when I doubled it? Give students a chance to turn and talk to their partner and describe as clearly as possible how the solid was doubled. Discuss students' observations and be sure students see that it is the side lengths—all of the side lengths—that were doubled.

Pose these questions: I doubled the side lengths, but is the new solid double the size? Is its surface twice as large as the smaller solid? Does it hold twice the volume? Ask, What would happen if we tripled it? Or quadrupled it? What patterns might we find? Would we find those same patterns in a different rectangular solid?

Explore

Provide small groups with snap cubes, grid paper (regular and snap-cube size; see appendix), isometric dot paper (see appendix), chart paper, markers, scissors, rulers, and tape. Ask groups to explore the questions:

- What happens to the surface area of a rectangular solid when you scale it up?
- What happens to the volume of a rectangular solid when you scale it up?

To explore these questions, groups construct a rectangular solid and then scale it up by a factor of 2, 3, or more. For each solid they construct, the group constructs a net of the figure on grid paper (see appendix) and draws the solid on isometric dot paper (see appendix). Students will need to find the surface area and volume of each figure and develop ways to organize all of their data to search for patterns. Groups develop a data display on chart paper, where they can tape their drawings of their solids, to look for and show the patterns they find. Encourage groups to explore more than one simple solid, such as starting with a $1 \times 1 \times 1$, $2 \times 2 \times 1$, and $3 \times 2 \times 2$.

During the work time, look for groups that organize their data using a table. Pause the investigation to show the class any tables that groups have created and highlight how useful these are for organizing data to see patterns. Encourage students to give this a try.

As students accumulate data, encourage them to look for patterns and develop ways of naming what those patterns are. Words, not just symbols, are entirely appropriate.

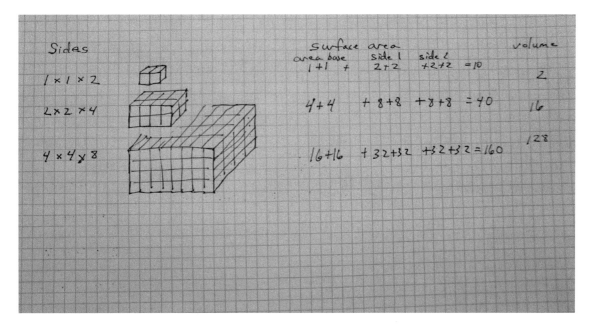

Student work showing their study of volume and surface area of a growing prism.

Discuss

Post all the groups' charts around the classroom. Do a gallery walk and ask students to look for connections between the solids other groups explored and the patterns that emerged. For instance, you might ask students, When the solids are different, are the patterns different or the same?

Discuss the following questions:

- What patterns did you notice as solids scaled up?
- How does the surface area change when you scale up a solid? How do you know?
- How does the volume change when you scale up a solid? How do you know?
- How can we describe these changes in words? What other ways could we express these patterns? (There is no need to get to symbolic notation, but some students may want to try.)
- Are these patterns true no matter what rectangular solid we start with? Why?

You might choose to use this discussion to introduce exponents as a way of recording the patterns of growth in volume and surface area. If you do, be sure to record the verbal ways students have talked about these patterns along with any other notation students tried, and connect these to *exponents* as a mathematical convention for showing quantities multiplied by themselves repeatedly. Tell students how we read exponents, such as "side length^2" is "side length squared." You might ask, Why does it make sense that we are using squared or cubic units in these patterns?

Extend

Invite students to investigate whether these patterns of growth in surface area and volume are true for other kinds of prisms, such as prisms with triangle or parallelogram bases. Students will not be able to construct these out of snap cubes, but they can create clear drawings using isometric dot paper and grid paper (see appendix) to explore other kinds of solids. Discuss what students find and why it makes sense.

Look-Fors

- **Are students scaling up their solids accurately?** Students may double only one side length or two, but the patterns we hope to investigate center on scaling figures by doubling and tripling all the sides. Ask students, How did you decide what the dimensions of the new solid would be? Also, remind students that they are exploring what happens when they scale up their original solid, so that each time they make a new solid they should be multiplying the side lengths of the *original solid* by 2, 3, 4, or more. Students may be tempted to double each solid in turn, or double the original solid, then triple that solid to make a new one. Doing this will certainly generate patterns, but will make the underlying patterns harder to identify. Remind students that the task involves returning to the original solid each time to grow it larger and larger.

- **How are students organizing the data they collect?** To see patterns in this complex investigation, students need to be tracking several measures at once, including the linear dimensions, the scale factor, the surface area, and the volume, along with any counting or calculations needed to find these values. This generates a lot of numbers, which can easily get muddled. Tables are a powerful organizational tool that enable us to see trends and changes across multiple dimensions at once. However, in our experience, students don't typically create tables without prompting. But learning to do so is critical to ongoing pattern searching in mathematics. In this activity, we've created some space and need for students to invent organizational structures, and we encourage you to look for innovative ways that students tackle this challenge that you can then share with the class so that the ideas might spread. We think this is more effective in seventh grade than simply providing students with a premade table template.

- **Are students seeing patterns?** If students do not have experience with exponential growth, they may not see patterns in the growth of the solids' surface area and volume. They may need more data to examine, and they may need to develop strategies they have never used before for looking for patterns. For instance, students may look for the difference between their original solid and their doubled solid by noting the change as addition or multiplication. Addition will not support noticing patterns, and multiplication gives a hint at a deeper pattern, if students have enough data. Students may begin to see a pattern only if they examine the change across several cases and then see that there is a pattern within the multiplication pattern. Ask, How is the surface area (or volume) changing? Zero in on changes from the original solid to each new scaled-up solid.

Reflect

Do you think these same patterns for scaling up a solid would be true for pyramids? Why or why not?

Seeing Proportional Relationships

Steve Strogatz is a wonderful mathematician, at Cornell; we feature videos of Steve in the University section of Youcubed, engaging students in inquiry-based mathematics teaching. He is also one of the world's leading mathematics communicators, sharing complex mathematical ideas in accessible and understandable ways. He writes for the *New York Times,* and he has written a number of books for the public, including *The Joy of x*. One of my favorite of Steve's books is called *Infinite Powers*; it is all about calculus. The book describes what calculus is, the big ideas inside calculus, and the reasons calculus is so important. Anybody teaching or learning calculus should read Steve's book. He points out that people could take an entire course in calculus and never gain the insights he writes about, as usually people are asked to perform the methods inside calculus and not stop to consider what calculus is. In his book, he writes about the beginning ideas inside calculus—linear relationships—with the example of a favorite food of his, cinnamon bread. Each cinnamon bread slice provides 200 calories, so one slice provides 200, two provides 400, and so on. He points out that we have learned, over time, to represent linear relationships on graphs, with the x axis showing one feature and the y another. In Steve's example (Figure 3.1), he uses the number of cinnamon bread pieces on the x-axis and the calories they provide on the y-axis.

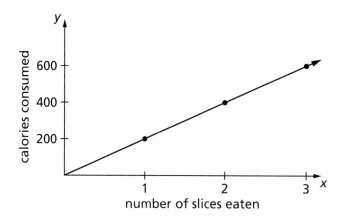

Figure 3.1   Graph showing calories eaten from slices of bread.
Source: Adapted From *Infinite Powers* (Advance reading copy), by S. Strogatz, 2019, Boston, MA: Houghton Mifflin Harcourt, p. 94.

When we plot them in this way, we see that they produce a linear relationship, as the points connect in a line. It is this straight line that tells us that the relationship between slices eaten and calories consumed is linear. It is typical for us to look at the relationships between two quantities by plotting them on a graph, and we do not think anything of it, but Steve writes that this was once a "radically transgressive" idea and that the ancient Greeks would have "screamed bloody murder" to see it. This is because they had only seen numbers as completely discrete quantities, not as connected by lines. Also, the two characteristics plotted—calories and slices—are completely different entities. When people did start to plot things that were connected by a linear relationship, they saw that they connected with a straight line. It was this visual insight that began searches into deeper connections, such as the nonlinear relationships that can be plotted as curves.

Linear functions are the beginning of thinking about a range of important ideas in mathematics, and they are the prelude to other sorts of interesting mathematical relationships and, eventually, as Steve's book shows, to calculus. Functions are critical to mathematics, and they are the topic of this big idea. In the different activities here, students will have an opportunity to think about and look for linear relationships and to show them visually.

In our Visualize activity, students are invited to plot lines to show different linear relationships in a ratio. We show a graph, but I would recommend not giving this to students; let them start their own. Why are the lines not parallel? The different ingredients each give linear relationships, but they are different ones, so each one has a different slope. Students are often introduced to slope in high school, as a formula. This is an opportunity to have students really understand slope. I would encourage a discussion with students about slope. What does the word mean? Students will probably come up with physical situations with different slopes, such as a wheelchair ramp or a mountain. These physical situations are good examples of slope in the world; if we plotted their height against their distance, we would have a straight line. We can also talk about the slope of relationships, such as the amount you pay for cups of coffee over a year, with each cup costing the same amount. When we plot the coffee cost, we will find a straight line, and that line has a slope.

In our Play activity, students are given different data sets to look at and are asked, Are they linear? Students explore four different data sets, hunting for proportional relationships. You can tell students that there are different relationships among this data, some of which are proportional and some not. It is their job to find them. Give students a chance to turn and talk about strategies they might use to determine proportionality.

In our Investigate activity, we show students two items—popcorn and pens—that are sold in different sizes, along with their prices. Students are asked first whether the prices are proportional to the sizes. They are then invited to brainstorm other items that come in multiple sizes and to investigate whether the prices are proportional or fair.

Jo Boaler

Reference

Strogatz, S. (2019). *Infinite powers: How calculus reveals the secrets of the universe.* (Advance reading copy). Boston, MA: Houghton Mifflin Harcourt.

Growing Dough

Snapshot

Students explore how tables and graphs can show proportional change in the ingredients of multiple batches of pizza dough.

Connection to CCSS
7.RP.2a,b,d, 7.NS.2c

Agenda

Activity	Time	Description/ Prompt	Materials
Launch	5 min	Show students the Pizza Dough Recipe sheet and tell them that sometimes families or restaurants want to make more than one batch so they can feed more people. Pose the question, How can we see that we are scaling up the recipe accurately?	Pizza Dough Recipe sheet, to display
Explore	30 min	Partners explore how to represent multiple batches of pizza dough ingredients in a table and a graph. Students consider how these displays help them see proportional relationships.	• Pizza Dough Table and Pizza Dough Graph sheets, one each per partnership • Ruler and colors, for each partnership
Discuss	15–20 min	Discuss how students constructed their graphs and how they might use the table or graph to make pizza dough. Discuss the patterns they notice, how these connect to proportional relationships, and how they may have supported students to catch errors.	

Activity	Time	Description/ Prompt	Materials
Extend	30–45 min	Students bring in the own recipes to explore what patterns they might see in the table or graph of multiple batches of ingredients. Discuss how these patterns are similar or different across recipes.	• Students' own recipes • Grid paper (see appendix), colors, and a ruler, for each group

To the Teacher

In this activity, we invite students to transform a recipe into proportional patterns in a table and a graph. Using a basic pizza dough recipe, we focus on three ingredients all measured in cups: flour, water, and oil. As the recipe is scaled up to create 2, 3, 4, or more batches, students organize the expanding recipe in a multicolumn table and a graph with multiple lines. These are complex tools, and students may not have experience constructing a graph with multiple lines or navigating a table with so many columns, while choosing which columns to attend to. Anticipate that students may struggle to think about how to organize and use all this data, and be ready to ask questions to help students think through their struggle productively.

One interesting observation that this exploration yields is that although the graph of each ingredient creates a line as the batches increase, the lines for multiple ingredients are not parallel. As shown in Figure 3.2, each line has its own slope, shaped by how much of each ingredient is needed in a single batch; flour, as the most abundant ingredient, has the steepest slope; oil has the shallowest slope. Talking about what students see in this graph and comparing the lines of proportional growth open up the opportunity to name the rate of change in the graph as *slope,* a useful concept for future work with linear relationships.

Activity

Launch

Launch the activity by showing the class the Pizza Dough Recipe sheet on the document camera. Tell students that this recipe makes enough dough for two pizzas, but sometimes families want to make more. If you worked in a restaurant, you'd want to make a lot more. But to make the dough work, you have to scale up the recipe so that you don't get dough that is too dry, too wet, or too oily. It's easy to make mistakes when scaling up a recipe—for example, by doubling one ingredient but not the rest.

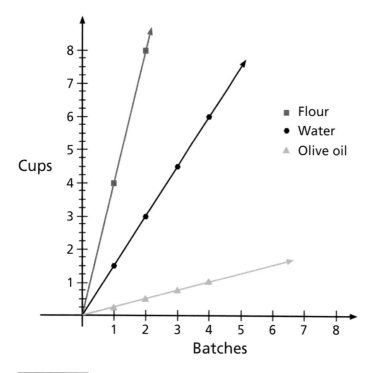

Figure 3.2

Tell students that today they are going to explore how they can scale up this recipe to make more and more batches of dough. Pose the questions, How can we see that we are scaling up the recipe accurately? How can tables and graphs help us see whether the ingredients are in proportion?

Explore

Provide partners with the Pizza Dough Table sheet, the Pizza Dough Graph sheet, colors, and a ruler. Ask students to extend the table and graph to show how much flour, water, and oil would be needed for more and more batches of dough. Students can choose whether to record 2, 3, 4, 5 batches and so on, or to try nonsequential batches such as 2, 4, 8, and so on. Encourage students to use color on the graph to color-code the different ingredients.

As students accumulate data in the table and graph, ask them to explore the question, What patterns do you see that tell you that the ingredients in each recipe are still in proportion?

Discuss

Discuss the following questions:

- How could you use your table or your graph to make pizza dough? How would you read it?
- What patterns did you notice in your tables and graphs?
- How can you see proportional relationships in your table?
- How can you see proportional relationships in your graph?
- Did you catch any errors using your graph or table? How did the table or graph help you identify an error?
- Why aren't the lines in the graph parallel? Does it matter for proportional relationships? Why or why not?

Extend

Invite students to find or bring in a favorite recipe and explore how to scale it up in a table and graph. Ask, How are the patterns similar to those in the pizza dough recipe? How are the patterns that you find different? Note that we deliberately chose a recipe where we could explore ingredients that used the same unit (cups). Students will need to decide whether they want to only examine ingredients that use the same unit, as we did, or whether they can invent ways of displaying data for recipes that use different units. Invite students to share what they create and compare the patterns of growth across recipes. Ask, What do you notice? How are the patterns across the recipes similar or different? Why might this be?

Look-Fors

- **Are students making a graph with multiple lines?** Students may not have experience constructing a graph with multiple lines and may not think that this is what is needed for this task. Rather than telling students this, you might encourage them to simply plot the points, using the symbols shown on the graph, and look for patterns before connecting the dots. This may help students see that there are three *patterns* being graphed. Alternatively, if you notice students connecting their data vertically, by drawing a line through all the points for a single batch, you might ask, What does this line show? Why are these points connected? How does this line show change as the batches grow? You might ask, What is changing as the number of batches increases? You might encourage students to focus on one ingredient at a time to help them see how lines could show change in that ingredient across batches.

- **Are students scaling up the original recipe?** As students add additional batches to their table, you'll want to pay attention to how they are thinking about the change. For instance, students could think about change accurately as adding a new batch of ingredients each time they add a batch, so that flour adds 4, water adds $1\frac{1}{2}$, and oil adds $\frac{1}{4}$ cup. They could also see this as a multiplication pattern, multiplying the number of batches by the original set of ingredients. However, students could see moving from one batch to two batches as doubling, which makes mathematical sense, unless students then think that they would double again to get three batches. Ask questions to clarify how students are thinking about growth so that it is truly proportional.

- **How are students labeling their *x*-axis?** We have intentionally not fully labeled the *x*-axis, so that students can grapple with how to do this. With one batch labeled, the scale is set, but students will need to think about what this scale is, how to build on it proportionally across the axis, and how to plot data matched to the correct number of batches. For instance, students might not make a table with consecutive whole numbers of batches (1, 2, 3, 4, . . .); they might instead do something patterned differently or not at all (such as 1, 2, 4, 6, 10). Students will need to think about how to label the axis so that it is consistent with the scale of the axis rather than matching their table. Without consistent labeling, students will not see the linear relationships embedded in the multiple batches of dough.

Reflect

Which was more useful for seeing proportional relationships, the table or the graph? Why?

Recipe: Pizza Dough

4 c flour
1½ c water
¼ c olive oil
1 packet of yeast
1 T salt

Pizza Dough Table

Batches	Cups of Flour	Cups of Water	Cups of Oil
1	4	$1\frac{1}{2}$	$\frac{1}{4}$

Pizza Dough Graph

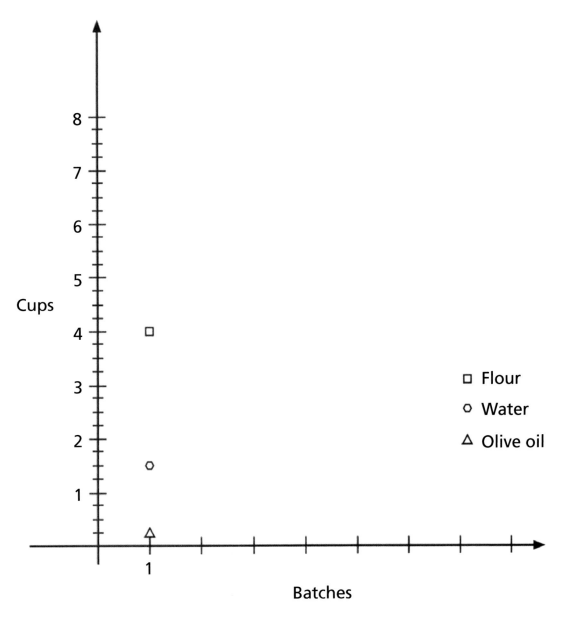

Cups

Batches

□ Flour
○ Water
△ Olive oil

Is It Proportional?

Snapshot

Students explore four different data sets, hunting for proportional relationships.

Connection to CCSS
7.RP.2, 7.RP.1, 7.RP.3

Agenda

Activity	Time	Description/ Prompt	Materials
Launch	10–15 min	Remind students of the ways they identified proportional relationships in the Visualize activity. Show students four data sets and discuss what they represent. Ask, Which of these do you think are proportional? How could you figure it out?	• Students' work from Visualize activity, to display • Playing with Data Sets sheet, to display
Play	30–45 min	Groups use tools to explore the relationships in the Playing with Data Sets sheet, looking for proportional data. Groups try to make generalizations about the data and predict data not shown.	• Playing with Data Sets sheet, one per group • Make available: grid paper (see appendix), colors, and rulers
Discuss	15–20 min	Discuss how students looked for proportional relationships, the patterns they found, the generalizations and predictions they could make, and the ways they displayed the data. Connect different ways that students generalized the patterns they noticed.	

To the Teacher

In this activity, we offer students the opportunity to play with four very different data sets: prices before and after sales tax, fence sections and posts, side length and area of square backyards, and animal gestation lengths and life spans. Moving between these very different data sets and making sense of what they communicate may be challenging for students. In the launch, we encourage you to spend the time needed to orient students to the data, define terms, and ensure that students comprehend the categories of data being compared. Another key challenge of exploring such different data sets is the very different numbers they use. If students use graphs as a way to look for proportional relationships, and we hope they do, they will need to make decisions about how to scale the axes to fit each type of data, including the price data, which is expressed in decimals. Students may struggle with these choices; consistently scaled axes are necessary to visualize proportionality, and they are worth the struggle.

Note that we have borrowed some of the animal data from Steve Jenkins's fabulous *The Animal Book*. This text and his book *Animals by the Numbers* are outstanding resources for data and show the patterns and variation that exist in the natural world.

Activity

Launch

Launch the activity by showing students the graphs they made of the pizza dough data in the Visualize activity and remind them of the work they did to identify the proportional relationships in this data.

Show students the four data sets they will be working with today on the Playing with Data Sets sheet and briefly describe what each is meant to represent. For instance, students may not know what "gestation length" means or be able to visualize a fence section. Be sure that students can imagine what each data set describes.

Tell students that there are proportional relationships among this data, and relationships that are not proportional. Ask, Which of these data sets do you think is proportional? How might you figure it out? Give students a chance to turn and talk about strategies they might use to determine proportionality.

Play

Provide each group with a copy of the Playing with Data Sets sheet. Make available grid paper (see appendix), colors, rulers, and any other tools students might request to explore the following questions for each data set:

- What patterns do you notice in the data?
- Which of these show a proportional (linear) relationship? How do you know?
- What generalizations can you make about the data?
- What predictions could you make about data that is not shown? How did you come to these predictions? How confident are you in them?

Discuss

Discuss the following questions:

- What patterns did you notice in the data?
- Which data sets were proportional, and how did you see that? What strategies did you develop for seeing proportional relationships?
- What generalizations can we make about the data?
- What predictions can we make about the data not shown in these sets? How did you come to these predictions? How confident are you in them?

Invite students to show the ways they have displayed the data to look for patterns and relationships. Be sure to point out that we can make justifiable predictions about data even when the data are not proportional. The lack of a proportional relationship may simply reduce our confidence in our predictions or make it challenging for us to generalize. Students' generalizations may be stated in words, shown with gestures, represented on graphs, or named abstractly with symbols. In the discussion, make connections between these different ways of describing patterns in the data.

Look-Fors

- **Are students reasoning about proportionality in the table?** While all the data can be explored visually through a graph, students may begin to notice clues in the table that support or refute a proportional relationship. For instance, the animal data reveals a general increase in life span along with an increase in gestation length, until you look at the humpback whale. A more careful look at the same data shows that a dog's gestation length is about three times that of a mouse, but a dog's average life span is 11 times longer. We include this data to encourage students to examine patterns both in the graph and in the table; be on the lookout for instances where students reason about the relationships in the table and make conclusions or predictions using this data. You'll want students to share these methods in the closing discussion.

- **How are students scaling axes when graphing?** As mentioned in the To the Teacher section, setting up four different graphs for these data sets is particularly challenging because the range of each set is very different. The fencing data has a small range with whole numbers, while the sales tax data is even smaller but includes decimal values. The backyard and animal data sets have large ranges for one set of values and a much smaller range for the other set of values. Each of these sets requires thinking through the labeling of the axes as a new and separate task. The axes need to be scaled consistently and able to include all the data. As they get started, ask students how they are thinking through setting up their graphs. You might ask, How do you know how to label the x- and y-axes? How will you make sure all the data can fit? What intervals make sense for this data? Notice whether students simply transfer the data over to the graph without scaling the axes. Draw attention to variation in the intervals and ask, What does this unit (one box on the graph) mean? You might want to pause the class to discuss axis intervals if you notice many groups struggling with consistent labeling. You could ask, Can you label the axes any way you want? Why or why not?

- **Are students distinguishing between proportional and predictable data?** Each of the data sets has a trend. One idea for students to explore in these data sets is the difference between data with a pattern and one with a proportional relationship. The square backyard data offers an opportunity for students to grapple with what makes a proportional relationship; this data is quadratic and predictable, but not proportional and linear. Help students think about what it means to be proportional by asking questions about why this data set is or is not proportional. Ask, What does it mean to be proportional? Support students in thinking about proportionality as consistent incremental change: for each unit of change in x, there is a fixed changed in y.

Reflect

What other proportional relationships in the world can you think of? How do you know they are proportional?

References

Jenkins, S. (2013). *The animal book*. Boston, MA: Houghton Mifflin Harcourt.

Jenkins, S. (2016). *Animals by the numbers*. Boston, MA: Houghton Mifflin Harcourt.

Playing with Data Sets

Paying Sales Tax

Price of Items	Total Price Paid
$5.50	$5.94
$7.00	$7.56
$12.00	$12.96
$15.00	$16.20
$16.25	$17.55

Building a Fence

Number of Fence Sections	Number of Posts Needed
2	3
3	4
5	6
12	13
26	27

Square Backyards

Length of a Side	Area of the Yard
4 m	16 m²
6 m	36 m²
9 m	81 m²
11 m	121 m²
18 m	324 m²

Animal Gestation and LifeSpan

Animal	Gestation Length	Average LifeSpan
Mouse	20 days	1 year
Dog	62 days	11 years
Black Bear	210 days	18 years
Human	266 days	79 years
Humpback Whale	350 days	45 years

Sizing Up Proportions

Snapshot

Is cost proportional to size? Students investigate pricing structures for items that come in different sizes to determine whether they are fair.

Connection to CCSS
7.RP.2a,b,d, 7.RP.1

Agenda

Activity	Time	Description/ Prompt	Materials
Launch	10 min	Show students two items—popcorn and pens—that are sold in different sizes, along with their prices. Ask, Are the prices proportional to the sizes? Brainstorm other items that come in multiple sizes and invite students to investigate whether the prices are proportional or fair.	• Sizing Up Proportions sheet, to display • Optional: chart and markers
Explore	40+ min	Small groups investigate pricing structures across multiple items to explore whether pricing structures are proportional or fair. If the pricing is not fair, students propose ways they would change it to be fair. Groups create charts to show their findings.	• Chart paper and markers, for each group • Grid paper (see appendix) and rulers, for each group • Make available: Sizing Up Proportions sheet, flyers, circulars, catalogs, and/or internet access

Activity	Time	Description/ Prompt	Materials
Discuss	15–20 min	Post groups' charts, clustered by proportional and nonproportional pricing relationships. Discuss the methods students used to determine proportionality, which pricing schemes they believe are fair and unfair, and how they would now approach buying in the real world.	

To the Teacher

The cost of an item should be proportional to the quantity of the goods, but this is rarely the case. People have come to expect a unit-rate discount for buying more. Sometimes the pricing structure is inexplicable, with a middle size being the most expensive. Exploring the relationship between price and size is at the heart of this activity. We have structured this investigation so that students can start with the two ideas we have provided and take their exploration in whatever direction their own interests lie. Students will need access to resources, such as online stores or print circulars or catalogs, for finding actual pricing data for the goods they care about.

Activity

Launch

Launch the activity by telling students that lots of things in the world are sold in different sizes. On the document camera, show students two examples of this from the Sizing Up Proportions sheet: movie theater popcorn and pens. Point out that for each size, there is a different price. Ask, Are the prices proportional to the sizes? Give students a chance to turn and talk to a partner about what they notice. Ask students to share their observations. Focus this brief discussion on the ways students are thinking about proportion and sizes.

As a class, brainstorm other things that come in different size sets or amounts. Students may mention anything from cellphone data plans to bottles of water. You may want to jot these ideas on the board or a chart as a reference. Pose the questions for the investigation: Are costs proportional to size? How can we tell? Are the prices fair? Why or why not?

Explore

Provide small groups with chart paper, markers, grid paper (see appendix), rulers, and access to product information, such as the Sizing Up Proportions sheet, flyers, circulars, catalogs, or online stores.

Groups explore situations where products come in different sizes and investigate the following questions:

- Are costs proportional to size? How do you know?
- Are the prices fair? Why or why not?
- If the prices are not fair, how would you change the prices to be fair?

Students can begin by investigating popcorn and pens if they wish. Then invite students to find different things that come in multiple sizes and to use rates, tables, pictures, or graphs (or Excel) to determine whether the prices are proportional to the size.

Challenge students to find some pricing structures that are proportional and some that are not. Groups make two charts showing their findings, sorting products by proportional and nonproportional pricing.

Discuss

Post the charts groups have created, putting the examples of proportional pricing in one space and those of nonproportional pricing in another. You may want to give students a chance to do a gallery walk to look at others' findings. Discuss the following questions:

- How did you decide whether pricing was proportional? What strategies did you use or develop?
- What products did you find that were priced proportionately? Which were not?
- Would you say the pricing patterns you found were fair or not fair? Why?
- What do your results tell us about how to make the best buying decisions?
- What are you wondering now about pricing in the real world?

Be sure to discuss the notion of fair pricing in detail. As noted in the Look-Fors section, *fair* can mean different things, and the class may legitimately not agree on what constitutes fair and unfair pricing. They do not need to come to agreement about this issue, but students should make clear how they were thinking it through. They may be able to agree more readily on examples of *unfair* pricing.

Look-Fors

- **Are students looking for comparable data?** In an investigation in which students have to generate their own data by looking at resources such as catalogs and online stores, it matters what data they select to compare. As you observe groups, look for whether students are comparing identical products (that is, the same brand and item) or products that may have other reasons for price differences (such as comparing gel pens to ballpoint pens). Also, are students looking at the pricing at a single store? Prices for a single item may vary from store to store and are only really comparable within a store. For instance, if students find a price for a pack of markers at an office supply store, they will then need to compare that price to smaller or larger packs of the same product at the same store. The idea that pricing can vary by store, brand, and product type may not be new to students, but they may not be thinking about the need to compare products consistently across these variables.

- **How are students looking for proportionality?** There are several methods students could use to assess whether pricing structures are proportional. Students might use unit rates for each size, for instance, or graph the prices against size and look for linearity. As you look at students' approaches, consider whether students are looking at the entire pricing scheme or are addressing proportionality as a yes-no question. For instance, students could find the unit rate for one package and then the unit rate for a second package; if the two rates were different, the group might stop there and simply say that the pricing for that item was not proportional. Although this approach is accurate, it means that students will lose insight into what the full pricing structure is and whether it might fit into a definition of *fair*. Further, looking at the data as a test (proportional: yes or no), means that it is harder to see patterns across products. For instance, students wouldn't be able to see whether larger packs typically have a lower unit rate, regardless of the item. Ask students, Do you want to see how all the prices for this item compare? Why might that be useful? Even if students stick to a yes-no approach, comparing these groups' data with the data from groups who assess all prices will make for interesting conversation in the discussion.

- **How are students conceiving of "fair" in pricing schemes?** We have deliberately asked students to consider both proportionality and fairness in this investigation to highlight why they may and may not be synonymous. Students should grapple with the questions, Is it fair that the unit rate goes down as you buy more? Or should it be constant? Or are all pricing schemes fair, as long as the customer knows how to evaluate them? As you circulate during the investigation, ask groups how they are thinking about what *fair* means. Push students to think about alternative interpretations as they develop their ideas. For instance, if groups think a constant unit rate (that is, a proportional relationship) is fair, you might ask, Would it be *unfair* if the price of the large pack were *lower*? If groups instead think it is fair that the unit rate decreases as the packs get larger, you might say, "The other way to think of that is that the unit rate goes up as you buy less. Is it fair that I have to pay more to get less?" There is obviously no clear definition of fair, but you want students to think critically about what fair could be.

Reflect

When deciding what size package of a product to buy, what will you be thinking about? How will you decide?

Sizing Up Proportions

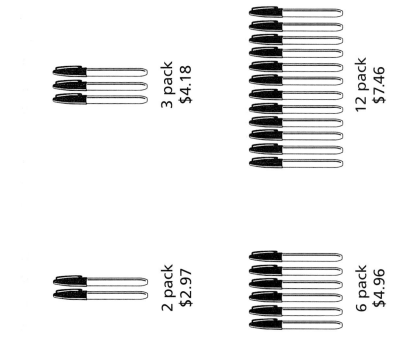

3 pack
$4.18

12 pack
$7.46

2 pack
$2.97

6 pack
$4.96

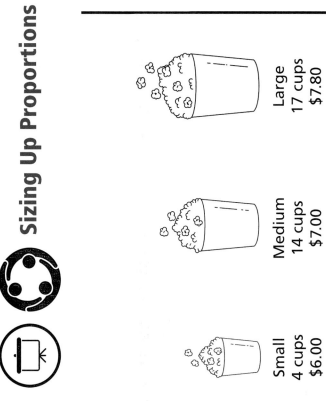

Large
17 cups
$7.80

Medium
14 cups
$7.00

Small
4 cups
$6.00

BIG IDEA 4

Understanding Percents in the World

A recent survey in the UK found that 20% of adults did not know how to use percentages. If my experience in life is anything to go by, the number of people confused by percentages may be much higher. Judging from conversations with many people—children and adults—it seems that they are not unclear about how to enact a procedure but rather are confused by the different uses of percentages that involve completely different calculations. The typical problem is that people do not know how to set up the calculation. Often when we help students, we skim over the differences between different uses of percentage and instead talk through what to do in each case. But it is the setting up of the method to use that is hardest.

The two main differences in the uses of percentage are these. In some situations, we need to calculate a percentage of something—for example, this sale item has 25% off its original price of $140. In that situation, we are calculating $\frac{25}{100} \times 140$. That calculation involves dividing by 100. But in other situations, we are told two values and asked questions such as, What is $\frac{30}{50}$ as a percentage? In that situation we do the opposite: we multiply by 100 ($\frac{30}{50} \times 100$ gives us 60%). If students only learn to perform calculations—sometimes dividing by 100 and sometimes multiplying by 100—but never stop to think conceptually about what is different in the two situations and why the calculations are different, they are bound to become confused. When they meet percentages in life, often people do not know which calculation to use.

In our Visualize activity, we ask students to first look at a Mondrian-style piece of art and determine the percent of each color for the painting. Our goal is for students to engage flexibly with number and percent and also connect percent to area. In the piece of art, the areas for the same colors are not adjacent, nor are they the

93

same size. This will encourage students to visually work through determining the whole and parts of the whole and then move to percent. This is important for later study in high school, and it is a common theme on standardized tests. Students are asked to work out their own methods. After working in groups, they will later share their methods and learn from each other. Afterward they will design their own work of art for others to study and enjoy.

In our Play activity, we ask students to fold pieces of adding machine tape that have been cut into proportional lengths. As students fold a length that represents fixed dollar amounts of $10 to $60, they mark out the percentages with equivalent folds. When students have completed their task and all of the strips have been posted, they can discuss their findings. Students should notice things such as 25% of $60 is equivalent to 50% of $30, and 50% of $30 is twice 25% of $30. The visual display and the opportunity for visual number talk discussions are at the heart of this lesson. Students can playfully work toward understanding percentages through visualizations.

In the Investigate activity, students continue building number sense and a flexible understanding of percentages. Students are often taught to learn percentages with words to remember, such as "is over of, equals percent over 100." There are, sadly, a lot of worksheets and YouTube videos encouraging students to compute percentages in these mechanical ways. Instead we ask students to consider some typical questions using their own methods, which they share. This activity builds off the previous lessons in this big idea. When students have worked through and shared their methods, the activity concludes by asking students to create a book, presentation, or some other product to help others, including adults, better understand percents. In doing this they will be encouraged to stand back and consider the big picture of percentages and the different ways in which people use them.

Jo Boaler

Painting Percents

Snapshot

Students analyze and design paintings to visualize percents as a portion "out of 100," and connect percents to decimals and fractions.

Connection to CCSS
7.RP.3, 7.EE.3

Agenda

Activity	Time	Description/Prompt	Materials
Launch	5–10 min	Show students the Mixed-Up Mondrian painting. Ask, What portion of the painting is each color? How could you figure it out? Give students a chance to talk about how they might start.	Mixed-Up Mondrian, to display
Explore	20–30 min	Using the Mixed-Up Mondrian sheet, partners explore how to find and describe the portion of the painting that each color represents.	Mixed-Up Mondrian (either full-color or wireframe version), one or more per partnership
Discuss	15–20 min	Discuss the portion of the painting each color represents and how students expressed these quantities. Name percents as "out of 100" and make connections between equivalent ways of describing portions. Students add percent labels to each of their colors.	Mixed-Up Mondrian, to display
Explore	30 min	Partners design their own painting, based on more or fewer than 100 pieces, such as a 5 × 5 or 20 × 20 grid. For each color they use, partners annotate their painting to show what percent of the painting the color is.	• Grid or dot paper (see appendix), for each partnership • Colors and ruler, for each partnership

Activity	Time	Description/Prompt	Materials
Discuss	20 min	Each partnership pairs up with another to share their paintings and the methods they developed for finding percents. Partnerships present the methods they heard from the other group. Discuss what made finding percents in these paintings hard and the methods students developed.	
Extend	45+ min	Using grid paper or a pixel art app, students create a pixel image and develop ways to find the percent of the image each color represents.	Grid paper (see appendix) and colors, or access to a pixel art app

To the Teacher

In this activity, we return to an image that we used in the fourth-grade book for exploring equivalent fractions. The Mixed-Up Mondrian is based on *Composition II* created by Piet Mondrian in 1921, using colors similar to the palette he used at the time. The structure of this adapted painting offers a particular opportunity for building ideas about percents. The entire painting is built on an underlying square grid, 10 units by 10 units. The 100 building blocks of the painting are not immediately apparent, but there are clues embedded in the image that students can use to infer this structure. For instance, the row and column of unit squares on two edges of the large black square show that it is a 4 × 4 square. To better understand the work that students will need to engage in for this task, we encourage you to try to decompose the image yourself so that you can see which colors are harder and what clues students will need to detect.

In the second part of this activity, we invite students to create their own images, built on a grid other than 10 × 10 or 100 units. Students will then have to extend their thinking about percents beyond counting units to thinking proportionately. We leave the number of units in the image up to students, but their choice matters for how challenging it will be to make these connections. Grids with 25, 50, 200, or 400 units will be more advantageous than grids with 144 or 81 units. To help them complete this task, you may want to explicitly give students choices about the kinds of grids they might use.

Finally, in the extension, we make the connection between the art we've explored and pixel art, used to create all digital images. If you have the capacity to provide students access to technology, we think using a pixel art app (many free apps are available for any platform you have) will make the task particularly engaging. This extension raises the mathematical challenge again, because there could be any number of pixels in the image. Challenge students to develop ways to find the percent of their image that each color represents and discuss why this is hard.

Activity

Launch

Launch the activity by showing students the Mixed-Up Mondrian (full-color version) on the document camera. Tell students that this is a painting inspired by the work of Piet Mondrian, who often painted with squares and rectangles of blue, red, yellow, black, and white. Ask, What portion of the painting is each color? How could you figure it out? Give students a chance to turn and talk to come up with some ideas about how to start.

Explore

Provide partners with copies of the Mixed-Up Mondrian sheet, either the color or the wireframe version. If you use the wireframe version, you'll want to continue to project the color version on the screen for reference. Groups explore the questions, What portion of the painting is each color? How do you know?

Students work to develop ways of finding and expressing the portion of the image that each color represents. Note that students will likely use a mix of fractions and decimals, and some students may use percents; all are fine at this point.

Discuss

Discuss the following questions:

- What portion of the painting is each color?
- How do you know?
- How did you describe the portion?

Invite students to share their diverse ways of finding and expressing these values. Name that when we talk about something as a portion "out of 100," these are percents. *Per* means "out of," and *cent* means "100." Draw students' attention to any equivalent values to emphasize that fractions, decimals, and percents can all mean the same thing. For instance, you might note the different ways students represented the portion of the painting that is blue to show that $40\% = \frac{40}{100} = 0.40 = 0.4$. Ask students to use this idea to add a new label to each of their colors to show what percent of the painting each color represents and that this is equivalent to their other representations.

Explore

Provide partners with colors, a ruler, and grid or dot paper (see appendix). Ask students to design a new painting that is not based on 100 pieces, like the Mixed-Up Mondrian, but on more or fewer parts, such as a 5×5 or 20×20 grid. Partners explore the question, What percent of the painting is each of the colors? Partners should develop an image and then annotate it to show the percent of the image each color represents.

Discuss

Pair groups up and ask each group to share their image and their methods with the other group. Be sure students explain the design they have created and how they thought about the percent of the painting that each color represents.

Invite each group to present the other group's work and explain how that group found the percent represented by at least one of the colors. This encourages students to listen carefully to each other so that they can fully explain the work to the class.

Discuss the following questions:

- What made it hard to find the percents?
- What interesting methods did you or others develop?
- How were your methods different from or similar to the methods you used in the Mixed-Up Mondrian painting?
- How could we use percents to compare the colors in paintings or across different paintings?

Extend

Paintings like the Mixed-Up Mondrian are not the only case where we can decompose an image into percents. Pixel art—and all computer images—are created using colors on a grid. Find some examples of pixel characters, scenes, or objects on the internet that you can share with students. Invite students to design their own pixel art and figure out the percent that each color in their image represents. Students can use grid paper (see appendix) and colors or a pixel art app to complete their design.

Regardless of the medium, students will need to annotate the image with how they found the percent each color represents.

Look-Fors

- **How are students connecting percents, decimals, fractions, and proportions?** Key to developing ideas about percents is to make explicit connections to ideas about portion and proportion that students already know. Students likely have a range of comfort with fractions, decimals, and rates, which is why it makes sense to take every opportunity to connect all of these forms together. You'll want to emphasize that if 40 out of 100 squares are blue, we can think of that as 40% or $\frac{4}{10}$ or as the rate "for every 100 squares, there are 40 blue ones." Students may make some of these connections implicitly when one partner wants to use decimals and the other a proportion to describe a color, and they agree to record them both. Be sure to name these as equivalent as you talk with students and in each of the discussions. The notion of rate or proportion will be particularly helpful as students move to the second exploration, because it will enable students to ask questions such as, "If for every 25 units, 6 are red, how many would be red for 100 units?"

- **Are students choosing painting structures that will enable them to extend their thinking about percent as a proportion?** As students begin to build their own paintings, the structure or size of the underlying grid matters for how challenging it will be to think proportionately about percents. Suggest that students try a grid similar to the Mixed-Up Mondrian's 10 × 10, perhaps half the dimensions (5 × 5) or double (20 × 20). This will make scaling the percents a matter of multiplying or dividing by 4, a relationship students are likely to recognize. If students use a grid that makes scaling difficult (for instance, 12 × 12), then consider presenting this dilemma to the class: How can you find the percent of the colors when the whole has 144 squares? See whether students can develop some ways of thinking proportionately about this conundrum without you providing a procedure. If students are stumped, post this question in the room for students to continue to think about as they move through this big idea.

- **How are students thinking about percent when the whole has more or fewer than 100 units?** Thinking proportionately requires students to see percents as a kind of rate. Ask students how they can use this rate to help them think about their paintings. Students may invent ways of scaling up or down percents by multiplying or dividing by an appropriate scale factor. You might support students in thinking about scaling up or down by asking, If the same picture you created was enlarged (or shrunk) so it looked just the same but had 100 squares, how many would be [a particular color]? Students may run into challenges if their paintings are larger than 100 units. For example, if a 20 × 20 painting has 35 yellow units, when students think proportionately they will find a decimal answer inside a percent. Students may be confused about whether this makes sense. We don't typically mix forms (for instance, we never embed a fraction inside a decimal), so you may need simply to tell students that, as a convention, it is accepted that decimals can appear inside of a percent.

Reflect

What is a percent, and why might it be useful?

Mixed-Up Mondrian

Inspired by *Composition II*, Piet Mondrian, 1921

Mixed-Up Mondrian: Wireframe

Inspired by *Composition II*, Piet Mondrian, 1921

Building Benchmarks

Snapshot

Students build understanding of benchmark percents by folding adding machine tape, and use this model to make connections between percents and money.

Connection to CCSS
7.RP.3, 7.EE.3

Agenda

Activity	Time	Description/Prompt	Materials
Launch	5 min	Show the Percents in the World sheet and brainstorm instances where students have seen percents connected to money.	Percents in the World sheet, to display
Play	30 min	Each group works with a strip of paper matched to a dollar amount and cut to proportion. Groups fold the strip to find 50%, 25%, 10%, 5%, and 1% of the strip and the dollar amount each represents. Students color-code and label their strips to show their findings.	• Adding machine tape, one (or more) strip(s) per group, cut proportionately to the dollar amount the strip represents • Colors, for each group
Discuss	20 min	Post students' strips in order from smallest to largest dollar value. Discuss the methods students developed for folding and for finding dollar values for each percent. Look for patterns across the different strips and record students' observations in a chart.	• Chart and markers • Space to post students' paper strips

To the Teacher

This activity requires preparing materials carefully so that students can make meaningful comparisons. Students use adding machine tape to represent a dollar amount; the strip then becomes the whole. Folding this whole will enable students to see the size of the portion that is 50%, 25% 10%, 5%, and ultimately 1%. Students connect these percents to money, which we often need to do in the real world when taking a discount, adding tax, or determining a tip. A larger idea can be explored by putting these strips in the same space. Students can see that the value of 50% depends on the value of the whole, and that, for example, 50% of $20 is half the value of 50% of $40. They can also see other patterns that can be useful for finding 1% or 10%. To make these larger comparisons possible, we suggest that you make each $10 increment a specific length, at least 1 foot, and $\frac{1}{2}$ meter is even better. This will make the strip for $50 and $60 quite long, but folding to see 1% requires a great length. Students may need multiple strips of paper as they work to get close to 1%. Offer them as many as they need; having a set rate for feet or meters per $10 will make cutting new strips for groups much easier.

This activity is just the first in thinking flexibly about percents. To support students in continuing to build number flexibility when working with percents, we highly recommend using the number talks designed by Cathy Humphreys and Ruth Parker in their excellent book, *Making Number Talks Matter*. Just as students needed opportunities to build number flexibility with whole numbers, they need to engage with rational numbers repeatedly, hearing one another's strategies and trying out patterns.

Activity

Launch

Launch the activity by showing students the Percents in the World sheet on the document camera. Tell students that in the real world we often have to think about percents and money at the same time, as in these situations. Ask, When have you seen percents and prices in the world? Give students a chance to turn and talk, and invite students to share some examples.

Tell students that today they are going to begin to explore how we use percents with money by using adding machine tape to represent dollar values.

Play

Provide each group with a length of adding machine tape and a different dollar amount ($20, $30, $40, $50, or $60, for example). Be sure that the length of the tape is proportional to the amount (see the To the Teacher section). Using the paper strip to represent the dollar amount they have been given, ask students to fold it to find 50%, 25%, 10%, 5%, and 1% of that value. Have students color-code their strip to show each percent and dollar value. When complete, the strips should clearly show the size of the portion that each percent represents and the equivalent dollar amount.

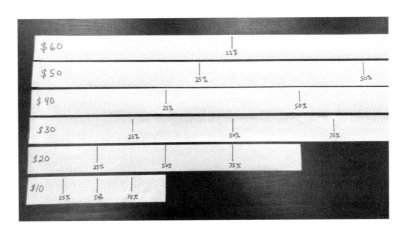

Adding machine tape cut in increments where 1 foot equals $10. The tape has been folded to show 25%, 50%, and 75%.

Discuss

Post all the strips on the wall or board in order of value, with the smallest on top and largest on bottom, making sure that their left edges align. Discuss the following questions:

- How did you fold your strip to find the percents?
- How did you use the folding to figure out the dollar value of each percent?
- (Give students a chance to study the board, paying attention to what other groups found.) What patterns do you notice across the strips?

Students may notice many patterns, for instance that 10% of $20 is $2, 10% of $30 is $3, 10% of $40 is $4, and so on. Record these patterns, along with examples, in a chart for students to refer to in the Investigate activity that follows. Be sure to draw attention to observations students make about the role that the whole plays, such as 25% of $20 is half the value of 25% of $40. Students should see that when the whole is larger, so are all the parts, and proportionately so.

Look-Fors

- **Are students connecting percents and folding to fractions?** In previous books, we have used folding adding machine tape as a way of exploring fractions. Students may also have folded paper in other kinds of activities to connect fractions to area. We explicitly used adding machine tape and its connections to both area and linear models to support students in making connections among these ideas and fractions. The percents students are exploring invite connections to fractions. For instance, students will find the conceptual work of folding and finding dollar values for 50% straightforward if they see 50% as equivalent to half. Similarly, 25% is half of that or $\frac{1}{4}$, and 10% is $\frac{1}{10}$, or the value you would get by dividing by 10. Making these connections is at the heart of this activity, and we encourage you to create space for students to discover and name them, rather than telling students to use these shortcuts.

- **Are students folding the entire strip or sections?** If students fold their strip in half and label it, then fold the entire strip in half again to get four sections of 25%, and proceed in this way through 1%, they will encounter a few challenges. First, their lines will become difficult to distinguish as the fold lines multiply. To address this, support students in thinking about how they could label or color-code the sections to show each percentage. They do not need to label all four sections of 25%; just one will do. You could also offer students multiple strips so that they have ones for 50% and 25%, another for 10% and 5%, and a final one for 1%. Second, their paper will become too thick to fold to get one 100 segments of 1%. Ask, How can you find 1% without making 100 parts? Students might discover that they could find 10% and then fold that portion into 10 segments, each 1%, for instance.

- **How are students connecting percents to dollars?** This dimension of the activity really begins to touch on finding a *percent of* something, or what we typically think of as multiplication. However, students are more likely to see it as dividing, because they are partitioning the whole value. Connections to unit fractions extend this thinking because we often conceive of finding $\frac{1}{4}$ or $\frac{1}{10}$ of a value by dividing by 4 or 10. Students may do this implicitly, and we encourage you to help make these connections explicit so that students can use them in the future. Most important, however, is that students continue to think back to the whole dollar value. They are not finding 10%; rather, they are finding 10% of $30. The importance of the whole needs to be emphasized whenever you discuss the methods students develop and their findings, because the value of any percent only makes sense when compared to the whole.

Reflect

How might you find 20% of a dollar amount?

Reference

Humphreys, C., & Parker, R. (2015). *Making number talks matter*. Portland, ME: Stenhouse.

What's It Going to Cost?

Snapshot

Students investigate how to use benchmark percents and patterns to find other percents in contexts such as sales tax, discounts, and tips.

Connection to CCSS
7.RP.3, 7.EE.3

Agenda

Activity	Time	Description/Prompt	Materials
Launch	10 min	Remind students of the work they did to find benchmark percents in the Play activity, and refer to their work if it is still posted. Tell students that they will explore how to use benchmarks to find other percents. Show situations for finding percents of a price and ask students to compare them.	• Students' work from the Play activity, as a reference • Two Uses of Percents sheet, to display
Explore	40+ min	Small groups use the situations on the Encountering Percents sheets or those of their own creation to investigate how to use benchmark percents to find the cost of items after tax, tip, or discount. Students develop methods and record their thinking.	• Encountering Percents sheets, for each group • Make available: adding machine tape, grid paper (see appendix), and rulers
Discuss	25+ min	Discuss the methods that work more effectively, how they might choose a method for a situation, and why these tasks were tricky.	

Activity	Time	Description/Prompt	Materials
Explore	60+ min	Groups design and create a product that teaches adults something important about thinking with and using percents in the real world.	Materials and tools appropriate to the products offered as options
Discuss	30 min	Groups present their products to the class and discuss the ideas and strategies the class deemed most important for adults to understand. Discuss the features of the products that were most effective for teaching ideas and how the products might be improved.	

To the Teacher

In this activity, we invite students to build on their work finding benchmark percents in the Play activity. Moving from benchmark percents to other percents, such as 7% or 30%, is a big shift, and students will benefit from a solid understanding of benchmark percents before diving in. Again, we recommend using the percent number talks found in *Making Number Talks Matter* (Humphreys & Parker, 2015) to build comfort and flexibility with percents both before and after this activity. To support students in moving from benchmark percents to those in this investigation, be sure to provide access to adding machine tape again so that they can fold it to think about how they might construct, for example, 30% by adding 25% and 5% or by finding 10% and tripling it.

We have designed the product of students' investigation to address a real need: deeper understanding of percents on the part of adults. Many adults struggle with using percents in the real world, in various situations such as estimating taxes and discounts, working out mortgage payments, and interpreting statistics in news articles. Restaurants frequently print references for tips at the bottom of receipts so that customers do not have to consider how to find 15% of the bill. The culmination of this investigation invites groups to create a product that they could use to help adults learn percents and be able to use them. Students might create a slide presentation, poster, pamphlet, video, or play. We encourage you to determine which options could work in your context and to offer students as wide a selection as possible.

This midworkshop interruption can provide just the sort of cross-pollination of ideas that students need to fuel extended work.

- **Are students struggling to connect benchmarks to the task?** This activity asks students to connect many ideas, including those from the Play activity, to do some challenging work with percents. If students seem to be struggling with all of the ideas embedded in the task—composing percents, finding the percent of a value, composing the percent of a value out of percent pieces, determining whether it is added or subtracted in the context of the situation, and ultimately finding the price—they may benefit from returning to adding machine tape to model the benchmarks for the dollar value they are working with in a single example. Once they have determined 50%, 25%, 10%, 5%, and 1% of, for example, $4, they might be better poised to use those components to find 8% tax on that value. You can support them in beginning to generalize a process by asking questions about how they used the benchmarks, so that students might then be able to try this in a different situation.

Reflect

Describe a situation in which you might need to find a percent of a cost, and then show how you can find the price you would pay.

Reference

Humphreys, C., & Parker, R. (2015). *Making number talks matter*. Portland, ME: Stenhouse.

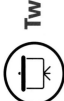

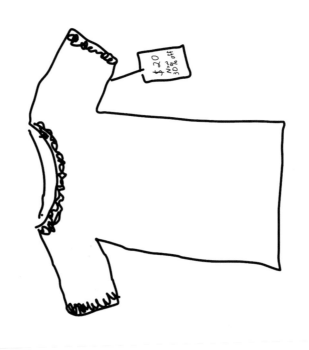

$6.00
7% sales tax not included

$20
now 30% off

How much money is a 16% tip?

Total $30.00

Sale Today 30% OFF

How much is the discount?

How much money is 8% sales tax?

Maths Poems By Jo Boaler $4.00

23% shipping charge not included

Shoes $40

How much is shipping?

Was $90
Now reduced by $36

What is the percent discount?

200.00

$25 from every $200 paycheck is put into savings. What percent of the paycheck is saved?

Mindset Mathematics, Grade 7, copyright © 2019 by Jo Boaler, Jen Munson, Cathy Williams.
Reproduced by permission of John Wiley & Sons, Inc.

What number is 37% of 550?	26 is what percent of 104?
34 is 20% of what number?	What number is 42% of 200?
56 is what percent of 28?	25 is 80% of what number?

Building Intuition about Probability

Students are likely to have been using ideas of probability since they were young. Every time they have talked about something being likely or unlikely, fair or unfair, they have used core concepts of probability. In this big idea, we intend for students to learn about and discuss ideas of fairness, likelihood, and uncertainty. It is nice to begin probability lessons with a discussion of the main idea—How certain is something to happen? You can ask students to come up with examples of things that are certain to happen today, impossible to happen today, and likely or unlikely to happen. They will probably enjoy coming up with examples. How likely, for example, is the principal to walk through your classroom door? What about a student? Or a giraffe?! Discussions of fairness are always interesting as well, and this is a topic students often feel passionate about, so some of our activities are designed to help them think about fairness.

When people come up with numbers to express probabilities, they sometimes use what they know about equally likely outcomes, and sometimes they use more complex thinking and statistical evidence. An example of an equally likely probability case is the flipping of a coin twice and getting two heads—we know that heads and tails are equally likely, so we can calculate probabilities. An example of a probability based on statistical evidence is in your phone weather app, where you might read that there is a 40% chance of rain tomorrow. An interesting discussion can be held with students about these different cases of probability. When can we work out probabilities? When do we need to collect evidence from trials or events to come up with probability estimates?

In our Visualize activity, students are given the opportunity to construct and consider different spinners and think about which of them are fair. The students will enjoy constructing their own spinners, and they will be activating important brain regions as they do so.

In our Play activity, we bring in another important manipulative when teaching probability—dice. There is much to be found out about the behavior of dice, particularly when rolling two or more and finding their total. Students will be able to discover that some numbers are more likely than others to be a result. When adding two dice, 1 is impossible and 12 is unlikely, but numbers such as 7 can be rolled in multiple different ways. After students have discussed the outcomes of two dice, they will be invited to roll three dice and both predict and collect the patterns that emerge.

In our Investigate activity, we begin to engage students in quantifying probability. In the previous activities, students were building intuition about and language for probability, with a focus on the likelihood of outcomes. This activity takes students into more precise ways of describing probability by asking, How likely is it? To consider this question, students work with bags of cubes, thinking about the likelihood of drawing out a particular color. Students will develop conjectures about the contents of the bags, using their probabilistic reasoning as they work.

Jo Boaler

Is It Fair?

Snapshot

Students build intuition about what makes a game of chance fair and connect chance to area by exploring spinner games.

Connection to CCSS
7.SP.5, 7.SP.6, 7.SP.7

Agenda

Activity	Time	Description/Prompt	Materials
Launch	10 min	Discuss the difference between games of chance and games of skill. Show students the Simple Spinner and the rules and ask, Is this game fair? Come to agreement about a definition of *fair* in games of chance.	Simple Spinner sheet, set up with spinner, to display
Explore	30+ min	Partners examine four spinners and the rules for each game, and make predictions about whether the game is fair or not. Partners test their predictions by playing the games repeatedly and gathering data.	• Spinners 1–4, for each partnership • Tape and paper clips, for each partnership
Discuss	20 min	Aggregate the data that partners have collected on charts for each spinner. For each game, discuss the predictions students made, whether the game is fair, and how the data influenced their thinking. Highlight probability language and connect chance to area.	Charts and markers, for collecting the class's data
Extend	45+ min	Partners construct their own spinners and game rules, making one that is fair and one that is not. Students test their designs. Discuss how students constructed their games.	Origami paper, paper clips, tape, and colors, for each partnership

To the Teacher

In this activity, we focus on developing intuition about what is fair, mathematically. In a game of chance, all players should win about the same number of times; that is, they should have the same chance of winning. Note the slight difference in these measures. Each player has the same chance of winning, but in practice that will mean that each player wins about the same number of times. The difference here is between experimental and theoretical probability, which students are not yet poised to name, but they may start to surface questions about this tension between theory and practice. All of this is in contrast to games of skill, in which players are unlikely to have an equal chance of winning because the outcome of the game is influenced by the different skills and experiences of the players. Most games that students play are neither entirely games of skill (such as chess) nor entirely games of chance (such as flipping a coin), but include a combination of skill and chance. As you introduce this activity, be sure that students can distinguish between game elements that are chance and those that are skill so that they can think about the concept of *fair* mathematically.

For the spinners in this activity, we have suggested that you use paper clips and our printed spinners. To do so, you partially unfold a paper clip so that one end points perpendicularly to the curved end. To make the spinner, poke the paper clip through the center of the paper spinner from underneath and tape it in place. You then drop a second paper clip onto the stem, which is able to rotate freely around it. For greater precision, you can unfold one part of this paper clip to make a pointer. These are cheap and relatively easy to make. If you want to avoid constructing spinners with paper clips, there are some useful spinner tools on the market. Transparent spinners can simply be overlaid on our examples and taped down for students to use repeatedly. Alternatively, stand-alone spinner arrows can be placed on top of our spinner sheets.

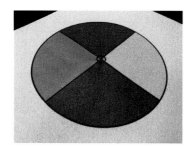

Unfold a paper clip and poke the end through the center of the spinner base.

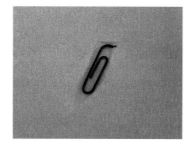

Use tape to attach the paper clip to the back of the spinner base.

Unfold a second paper clip and use it as the spinner.

Activity

Launch

Launch the activity by telling students that they are going to be exploring games of chance. These are different from games of skill. In a game of chance, there is nothing the player can do to change their opportunities to win. By contrast, in a game of skill, the use of knowledge, strategy, or skills can shift the outcome. You might ask students to share some examples of games of chance and games of skill to make sure that the class sees the distinction between these two classes of games.

Show students the Simple Spinner, set up with a paper clip (or other) spinner, on the document camera. Tell them that in this game of chance, a spin of red means that Player A wins, and a spin of blue means that Player B wins. Ask, Is this a fair game? Why or why not? Give students a chance to turn and talk to a partner about their reasoning. As a class, come to agreement about a definition of *fair* in the context of games of chance. Chart this definition for all to use as a reference.

Explore

Provide partners with copies of the Spinner sheets 1–4, tape, and paper clips. Show students how to use paper clips to construct spinners. For each of these games, partners read the rules carefully and predict whether it is a fair game or not. Students record their prediction and reasoning on the Spinner sheets.

Partners then test their predictions by playing the games as many times as they think is useful. Students collect data to determine whether the games are fair. Students consider the following questions:

- How many times do you need to play the game to decide whether it is fair?
- Is the game fair? How do you know?
- Were any of your predictions proven false? If so, why do you think that is?

Discuss

Aggregate the data that partners have collected by making a chart for each of the spinners and asking students to contribute their data.

Discuss the following questions for each of the spinners:

- Did you predict that this game would be fair? Why or why not?
- Is the game fair? Why or why not?
- Did putting the data together change your ideas about whether the games were fair? Why?

Students will be searching for words to describe what they have seen and how they are thinking about fairness. As probability words arise—such as *chance* or *more/less/equally likely*—slow down the conversation and be sure to highlight the words and what these words mean. Be sure to discuss how students were thinking about chance connected to the area of the spinners and the rules for the game.

Extend

Provide partners with origami paper, tape, paper clips, and colors. Ask students to make their own spinner games—one in which the game is fair and one in which the game is not fair. Students can construct their own spinners by folding the origami paper into regions. When unfolded, these spinners may need to be taped down for the paper clip to spin properly. You might challenge students, Can you create one spinner with two different sets of rules, where one set of rules makes the game fair and one set of rules makes the game unfair? Invite students to test their games to confirm whether they are fair or not. Discuss how students constructed spinners and rules for fair and unfair games.

Look-Fors

- **Are students connecting chance to area?** Area is key to building intuition about chance in games that involve spinners, and, ultimately, area can be used as a tool to model probabilities. Listen for how students are talking about the chance of winning based on how large the wedge(s) are on the spinner. Students may make claims that involve saying that a color is larger. Ask students to get precise by asking something such as, When you say "larger," what do you mean? Support students in naming that it is *area* that determines how likely a result is when spinning. This gets trickier when the areas (wedges) are not adjacent. Students will need to develop strategies for considering how to compose and compare these portions on the spinners. Ask them to describe how they did this, what they were seeing in their minds, or how they were decomposing the parts to see units.

- **How are students thinking about both the rules and the spinner?** In each of these games, there is an interplay between the design of the spinner and the rules for winning. A single spinner may be fair or unfair depending on the rules. Students will need to consider how the rules determine how much area is allotted to each player. Listen for how students describe the area of the spinner and connect that area to the rules for winning the game. Push students to articulate the role of the rules by asking questions about spinners that are equally divided, such as Spinner 1. You might say, "This spinner is divided into equal parts. Doesn't that mean it's fair?" to engage students in discussion about the relationship between the spinner and the rules. Be on the lookout for students who ignore the rules and focus only on the spinner. Draw their attention to the rules and ask them how the rules and the spinner help them think about fairness. These may be groups where their prediction and data disagree; it's okay to let students discover that they have made a mistake. This can make for an interesting case to discuss at the end.

- **How much data do students think is enough?** There is no precise answer to the question, How much data do I need? However, we do want students to be thinking about this question as they test their predictions. Students should be able to agree that only a few trials are not enough. For instance, students will likely recognize that spinning once won't tell you whether a game is fair and that more repetitions are needed. But are 4 spins enough? 10? 12? 20? Ask students, How will you know when you have enough data? Look for groups who make decisions after a very small number of trials, such as a group that spins Spinner 3 three times and decides on its fairness based on whether Players A, B, and C each win once. There is always a difference between theoretical probability (what we would expect by looking at the spinner and the rules) and the experimental probability (what happens when probability comes to life in the real world). That difference gets smaller with the more data, or trials, you have. You might help students think about this by asking them to consider an example such as the following: If a two-player game is fair, does that mean that both players are going to win exactly the same number of times? Does it mean that they will alternate who wins, Player A then Player B? Why?

Reflect

How can you decide whether a game of chance is fair?

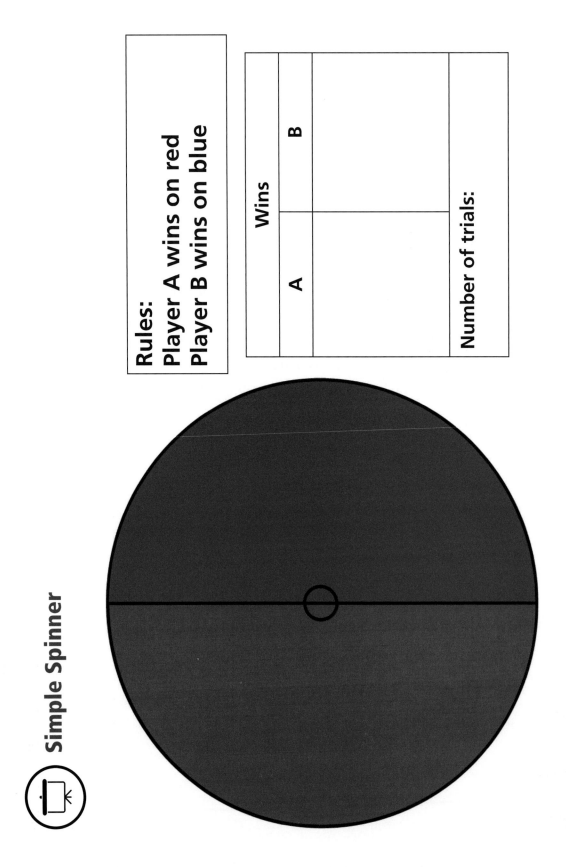

Simple Spinner

Rules:
Player A wins on red
Player B wins on blue

Wins	
A	B

Number of trials:

Spinner 1

Spinner 1

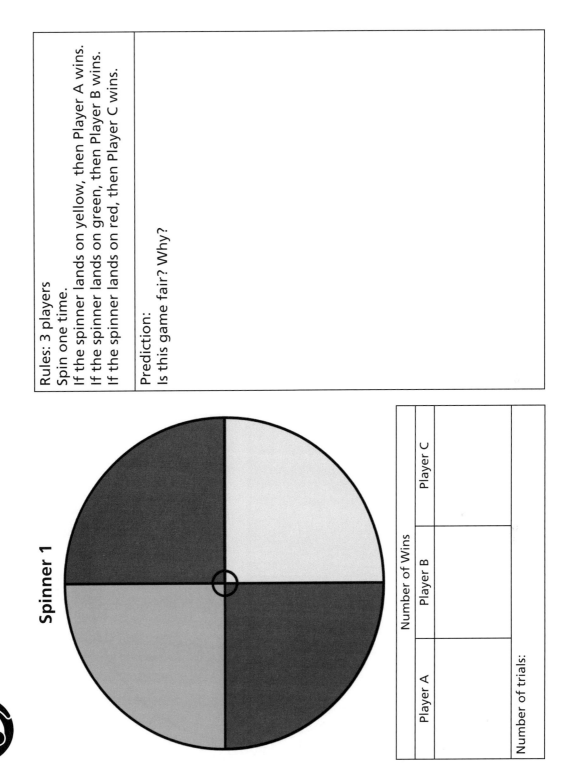

Rules: 3 players
Spin one time.
If the spinner lands on yellow, then Player A wins.
If the spinner lands on green, then Player B wins.
If the spinner lands on red, then Player C wins.

Prediction:
Is this game fair? Why?

Number of Wins

Player A	Player B	Player C

Number of trials:

Spinner 2

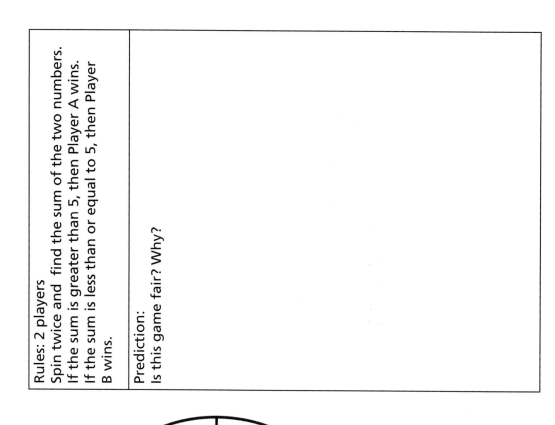

Spinner 2

Rules: 2 players

Spin twice and find the sum of the two numbers.

If the sum is greater than 5, then Player A wins.

If the sum is less than or equal to 5, then Player B wins.

Prediction:

Is this game fair? Why?

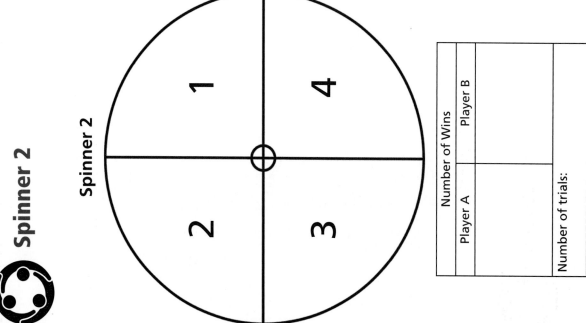

Number of Wins	
Player A	Player B

Number of trials:

Spinner 3

Rules: 3 players
Spin one time.
If the spinner lands on yellow, then Player A wins.
If the spinner lands on green, then Player B wins.
If the spinner lands on red, then Player C wins.

Prediction:
Is this game fair? Why?

Spinner 3

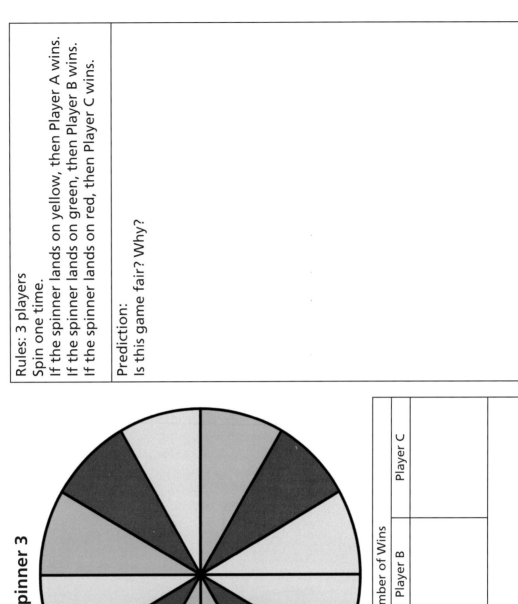

	Number of Wins	
Player A	Player B	Player C

Number of trials:

Spinner 4

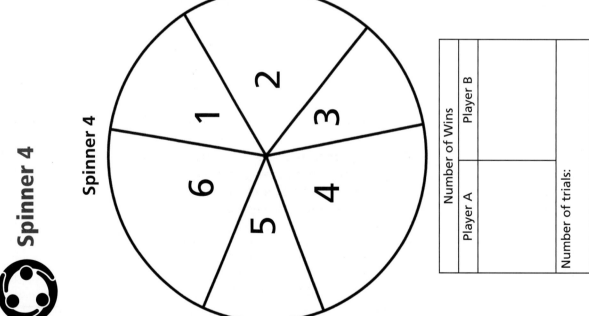

Spinner 4

Spinner segments: 1, 2, 3, 4, 5, 6

Rules: 2 players

Spin twice and find the sum of the two numbers.

If the sum of the values is odd, then Player A wins.

If the sum of the values is even, then Player B wins.

Prediction:

Is this game fair? Why?

Number of Wins	
Player A	Player B
Number of trials:	

Fair Sums?

Snapshot

When rolling a single die, all outcomes are equally likely. What happens when you roll two or more dice and find the sum? Students explore the shape of probabilities by experimenting with rolling multiple dice.

Connection to CCSS
7.SP.5, 7.SP.6, 7.SP.7

Agenda

Activity	Time	Description/Prompt	Materials
Launch	5–10 min	Show students a die and ask them whether all of the numbers are equally likely to be rolled. Come to consensus about the fairness of the die. Tell students that many games involve rolling two dice. Pose the question, When rolling two dice, are all of the *sums* equally likely?	Dice, two to display
Play	20 min	Partners explore whether the sums of two dice are equally likely or not by experimenting with rolling dice and collecting data. Students develop ideas about why the patterns they observe exist.	• Dice, two per partnership • Make available: grid paper (see appendix)
Discuss	15 min	Discuss the patterns students discovered, how they organized their data, and what might be leading to these patterns. Invite students to hypothesize about what patterns they might see when rolling three dice.	
Play	30 min	By rolling dice and collecting data, partners explore whether the sums of three or more dice are equally likely. Students develop ways of organizing and displaying data to help them see patterns.	• Dice, three or more per partnership • Make available: grid paper (see appendix)

Activity	Time	Description/Prompt	Materials
Discuss	15–20 min	Discuss how students organized their data, the patterns that emerged, the shape of the data, whether all sums are equally likely, and what might explain these results. Focus on how different ways of organizing the data enable students to see different patterns.	

To the Teacher

This lesson challenges students to develop ways to organize and display data to look for patterns. Students may need support and ideas.

Activity

Launch

Launch the activity by showing students one die and asking, If I roll this die, are all the numbers equally likely? Give students a chance to turn and talk to a partner, and then collect student responses. If students don't agree, you can conduct a class experiment with one die and collect data to support the notion that all of the numbers are equally likely.

Tell students that a lot of games rely on rolling two dice and adding the values of each die together. Pose the question, Are all of the sums of two dice equally likely?

Play

Provide partners with two dice, and make grid paper (see appendix) available. Ask students to explore the following questions:

- When rolling two dice, are all sums equally likely? Why or why not?
- If all sums are not equally likely, what sums are more likely? Why?

Invite groups to collect and organize data in any way they devise to support their exploration of these questions and the development of some ideas about whether all sums are equally likely.

Discuss

Discuss the following questions:

- How did you collect and organize your data?
- What data displays were most useful? Why?
- What did your data show you? Are all the sums equally likely?
- Why are the sums equally likely or not? What is happening with the dice that leads to these outcomes?
- What do you think would happen with three dice? Why?

Be sure to draw attention to the apparent contradiction in rolling two dice: each die has equally likely outcomes, but all sums of the two dice are not equally likely. Support students in reasoning about this contradiction and making sense of it based on what happens with the dice. That is, each combination is equally likely (for instance, there is the same chance of rolling a 1 and 4 as there is rolling a 3 and 2), but there are more combinations that make 7 than 2 as a sum. Grappling with this idea in the discussion will support students in predicting what might happen when rolling even more dice. Here we share a table that shows the different sums that are possible. Note that there are a lot more ways possible to make a sum of 7 than a sum of 11.

+	•	••	•••	•• ••	••• ••	••• •••
•	2	3	4	5	6	7
••	3	4	5	6	7	8
•••	4	5	6	7	8	9
•• ••	5	6	7	8	9	10
••• ••	6	7	8	9	10	11
••• •••	7	8	9	10	11	12

This table represents the sum of two dice rolls. There are six ways to make 7 and two ways to make 11. There are 36 possible number combinations.

Play

Provide partners with three (or more) dice and access to grid paper (see appendix) or other tools for organizing data. Students explore the following questions:

- What sums are possible?
- What patterns emerge if you roll and find the sum of three dice? Or more?
- Are all sums equally likely? Why or why not?
- What is the shape of the data when rolling three or more dice repeatedly?
- What outcomes are more likely? Why?

Again, students develop their own ways of collecting, organizing, and displaying the data from rolling and finding the sum of three or more dice. Invite them to consider the displays shared in the previous discussion and try something new.

Discuss

Invite students to share their findings and how they organized their data, using the document camera. Discuss the following questions:

- Are all sums equally likely? Why or why not?
- How did you organize your data? What strategies for organizing helped you see patterns?
- What is the shape of the data?
- What outcomes are more likely? Why?
- What is happening with the dice that creates these patterns?

Focus part of the discussion on the ways that students organized and displayed their data, and how these displays allowed them to see patterns. Some displays, such as graphs, will enable students to see the shape of the data, while others, such as tables, make these patterns harder to visualize.

Look-Fors

- **How are students organizing their data?** There are two types of representations students might choose: tabular and graphical. Tables typically make sense as a data collection tool, and students might organize possibilities and tally their findings as they roll dice. If the table is organized with the values in ascending or descending order, rather than mixed up, then the table can be used to see patterns. Students would likely be able to see that there are a larger number of rolls in the center of the set of possible outcomes than at either end.

However, graphs make visualizing data much easier, and students' inquiry would benefit from displaying the data from the table in a graph. Notice groups who are using only tables and ask them questions such as, How does your table help you see patterns? Is there any other way you could display the data so you can see patterns more easily? Look for groups who have developed graphical representations and be sure to highlight different forms in the discussions so that students might try new ways of visualizing the data.

- **Are students seeing the contradiction between rolling one die and multiple dice?** We want students to be curious about this phenomenon, and we hope that you will provoke that curiosity by asking lots of questions about why it happens. Students may take it for granted that rolling a die generates equally likely outcomes, so rolling two dice and finding the sum should be no different. When the data they collect diverges from this expectation, push students to investigate why it happens. Some students may have an intuition, perhaps stemming from playing many board games, that rolling a 6, 7, or 8 is more common that rolling a 2 or 12. They may predict that the outcomes are not equally likely, but, again, why would this happen? By pressing these questions, you can support the students in articulating the difference between the outcome as the sum (such as 8) and the outcome as the combination of values rolled (such as 3 and 5).

- **Are students using the language of probability?** This activity extends the use of probability terms that emerged in the Visualize lesson, such as *more/less/equally likely* and *chance*. Here we begin to use the language of *outcome*, as the result of an *event*, such as rolling a die. Listen for opportunities to provide students with precise words to describe the activity they are investigating and what they are noticing in the data. Students may be searching for words to communicate an idea, and these are prime moments to support students to name their own ideas with mathematical language and for them to learn new words when they need them, which helps them communicate with greater precision. If students use this language in discussion with a partner or the class, be sure to highlight the use of words that you hope others will take up in their own explanations.

Reflect

Rolling two dice involves chance, not skill, but not all the sums are equally likely. What other examples can you think of where the outcome is a matter of chance, but not all the outcomes are equally likely?

What's in the Bag?

Snapshot

Students explore bags of colored cubes to predict their contents. Groups try to name how likely it is to draw a blue cube from the bag, inventing ways of quantifying probability.

Connection to CCSS
7.SP.5, 7.SP.6, 7.SP.7

Agenda

Activity	Time	Description/Prompt	Materials
Launch	10 min	Show students one of the bags of cubes and tell them that inside are colored cubes, but we don't know how many or what colors. Invite students to draw out one cube and use that to make a prediction about the contents of the bag. Repeat this process to show how more data increases confidence in predictions.	Prepared bag of cubes, any one from the set made for the class
Explore	30+ min	Groups explore multiple bags of cubes and try to make a conjecture about the contents of each. Students may draw out one cube at a time, replacing it before drawing the next.	Several prepared bags of colored cubes (see To the Teacher section for details)
Discuss	20–30 min	For each bag, discuss groups' conjectures about the contents, how students arrived at their ideas, and how these predictions compare. Reveal the contents of each bag and compare the contents to the conjectures. Discuss the methods that proved most accurate.	Several prepared bags of colored cubes (see To the Teacher section for details)

Activity	Time	Description/Prompt	Materials
Explore	45+ min	Students play a game with the bags in which a player wins when they draw a blue cube. Groups explore the question, What are the chances of winning for each bag? How can we put the bags in order from least to most likely to win?	• Several prepared bags of colored cubes (see To the Teacher section for details) • Bag Cards, to match the prepared bags, for each group
Discuss	20+ min	Draw a line from impossible to certain and invite groups to add Bag Cards one at a time to the line, justifying the placement of each. Support students in developing quantitative ways of justifying how likely it is to draw a blue cube from each bag. Compare the results to the experiments students conducted earlier and discuss why they are not identical.	• Bag Cards, one class set • Tape, magnets, or pushpins for posting the cards

To the Teacher

To prepare for this activity, you'll need to assemble several bags of cubes. The bags need to be opaque and easy to reach into without looking at the contents, such as drawstring bags, paper lunch bags, or socks. You'll want to have at least one bag per group, though you could have more for the class to explore. Construct the bags so that they range in the total number of cubes and the number of blue cubes, which, in the second half of the investigation, will be the winning cubes. You'll want to choose some combinations for which the probabilities of drawing a blue cube are similar, and you'll want one bag where the probability is 1 (certain, or 100%) and one bag where it is 0 (impossible, or 0%). Here are some suggested bags for you to select from:

15 cubes: 15 blue
12 cubes: 11 blue and 1 red
20 cubes: 15 blue, 4 yellow, and 1 red
10 cubes: 5 blue and 5 yellow
12 cubes: 5 blue, 4 red, and 3 yellow
20 cubes: 8 blue, 8 red, and 4 yellow

15 cubes: 3 blue, 6 red, and 6 yellow

8 cubes: 2 blue, 4 yellow, and 2 red

10 cubes: 1 blue, 6 yellow, and 3 red

14 cubes: 8 red and 6 yellow

These distributions are provided on cards for you to cut out so that students can use them in the second half of the investigation as they try to sort them by the probability of drawing a blue block. Notice that each bag is given a letter label on the cards. You'll want each of your bags to have a letter label so that students can refer to the bags and compare conjectures for the same bag. If you make your own bags, you'll need to make your own cards to match.

The big push in this activity is figuring out ways to quantify probability. In the previous activities, students built intuition about and language for probability, with a focus on more, less, and equally likely outcomes. This activity bridges students into more formal and precise ways of describing probability by posing the question, *How likely is it?*

Activity

Launch

Launch the activity by showing students one of the bags of cubes and telling them that inside are a bunch of colored cubes. Tell students that, without looking, we don't know what exactly is inside the bag. We don't know how many cubes there are or what color they are. In today's investigation, the goal is to figure out what's in the bag, and to do that we are allowed to take one cube out at a time, look at it, and then put it back.

Invite one student to draw a cube out of the bag and show it to the class before replacing it. Ask the class, What do you think is in the bag? Why? Give students a chance to turn and talk to a partner, then take some ideas from students. Students will likely say that seeing one block isn't enough to know what is in the bag. If so, invite another student to draw another cube to show to the class and replace it. Repeat the question, What do you think is in the bag? Why? Discuss how this second draw gives more information, but not enough to be confident.

Tell students that today they are going to be exploring a bunch of bags and using this one way of gathering data—drawing and replacing cubes—to develop conjectures about what's in each bag.

Explore

Provide one bag of cubes (see the To the Teacher section) to each group. Tell students that each bag contains cubes. Ask groups to develop their best conjecture about the number of each color cube that is in the bag. To do this, groups may draw out cubes one at a time, but after each time, they must replace the cube in the bag. Note that students will likely feel the cubes to count how many there are; this is entirely appropriate as long as they are not looking at the contents.

Rotate the bags from group to group so that each group has a chance to develop ideas about each bag. Groups should keep a record of the data they collect for each bag, and label that data so they know which bag it came from.

Discuss

Discuss the following questions for each bag in turn:

- What are your conjectures about the contents of the bag?
- How did you arrive at your conjecture?
- How confident are you in your conjecture? What could you do to increase your confidence?
- How do our conjectures compare? Which do you think are most accurate? Why?

As you discuss the different bags, students may suggest combining their data to make their conjectures more accurate. If they do, support students in trying this and then comparing the results to the groups' individual conjectures.

After you discuss each bag, open the bag and show the class the contents. The document camera works well for this. Discuss the following:

- Which conjectures were closest?
- What does this tell us about effective methods?

After you have discussed all of the bags, ask students these questions:

- What methods helped us get closest when making conjectures about the contents of the bags?
- Why do you think these worked?

Explore

Tell students that they are going to explore a game with these bags. In this game, players take turns drawing a cube out of the bag and replacing it. A player wins if they draw out a blue cube.

Groups explore the following questions:

- What is the chance of winning for each bag? How do you know?
- How can we put these bags in order from most likely to win to least likely to win?

Provide each group with access to the bags and a set of Bag Cards to match the bags your class explored. Groups can use these cards for information and to literally arrange them in order from least to most likely.

Discuss

Draw a horizontal line on a board, labeled *impossible* on one end and *certain* on the other, where students can post the cards from least to most likely. Invite each group to place one card on the board and to explain why they are placing it there. As each group places a card, they need to explain its position on the line and its position relative to the other cards. You might ask these questions:

- How did you decide where to place the card?
- Why do you think it is more (or less) likely than the card next to it?
- How likely is it that a person will draw a blue cube from that bag? How do you know?

The central goal of this discussion is to support students in finding ways to describe probability with numbers, whether they use language such as *40%*, $\frac{4}{10}$, or *4 out of 10*. When discussing bags with a similar probability of drawing a blue cube, students will need to work to justify one or the other as more likely. These cases encourage quantifying probability in some way. Spend time discussing these cases to draw out ways of accurately comparing the probabilities of drawing a blue cube.

Ask students, How do these probabilities compare to the data you collected earlier? Depending on the sample size, these probabilities should be close to, but not exactly, what students found. You might take this opportunity to name these as *experimental probability,* or the probability of an event found through simulating that event, and *theoretical probability,* or the probability of an event found through calculating the possible outcomes. These two forms of probability should be close, which is to say that the theoretical probability predicts what is likely to happen in life, but they are rarely identical. You might ask students why they think that is.

Look-Fors

- **How are students connecting their data to their conjectures?** As students collect data about each bag, they have the opportunity to make connections between that data and a prediction about the bag's contents. Students may try to do this quite literally, by drawing out 10 cubes one at a time and then predicting there are 10 cubes composed of their exact results. This strategy can enable students to form one kind of prediction, provided there are actually 10 cubes in the bag, but a more precise prediction could be made by drawing cubes 20 or 30 times. If they do this, students will need to think proportionally about the contents. If they feel that there are 15 cubes in the bag and draw cubes 30 times, they might halve their results to make a prediction. This would be more accurate, and could also lead to an impossible prediction that there are $4\frac{1}{2}$ blue cubes. If you notice this kind of thinking, be sure to draw attention to the value in the larger number of trials and the proportional reasoning the students were employing. You might then ask, Do you really think there are $4\frac{1}{2}$ blue cubes in this bag? If that's not possible, what prediction could you make from your data that is possible?

- **Are students finding chance by experimenting or by analyzing the bag's contents?** In the second half of the investigation, we invite students to compare the probabilities of drawing a blue cube out of each bag. Our intention is to encourage students to develop ways to quantify probability, and students may do this in one of two ways. Students may simply conduct the experiments again, collecting data to see which bag wins more often. Or students may analyze the content of each bag and compare the chances of drawing a blue cube based on the number of cubes in the bag. Both can lead to defensible conclusions, but only an analytic approach can lead to consistent, precise results. Experiments change depending on the particular trials and how many you choose to conduct. To encourage students toward an analytic approach, you might ask students who are experimenting, Do you think your results will always be true? How confident are you that one bag is more likely than another? You might encourage students to focus on two bags for which you know the probabilities of drawing a blue cube are close to one another. The only way to be confident about these bags is to focus on the contents.

- **How are students describing the chances of drawing a blue cube?** There are many ways students might quantify the chances of drawing a blue cube. Students may use fractions, decimals, ratios, percents, or language, such as "1 out of 10" or "impossible." All of these are valid ways of describing probability. The key is to make connections between these various forms so that students can see that they are equivalent, and they can make decisions about which form they think makes the most sense for expressing or comparing probability. For instance, "2 out of 8" or $\frac{5}{12}$ can be completely accurate ways of expressing probability, and they have the added benefit of potentially naming the number of cubes in the bag as well as how many are blue. But these forms can make *comparing* probability challenging; decimals or percents make this task much easier, even if they obscure the number of cubes in each bag. Encourage students to quantify the probability by asking, How likely is it? Then ask students, How will you compare these two bags to know with confidence which one is more likely to win?

Reflect

Design a bag of colored cubes. What is the probability of drawing each color in your bag? How do you know?

Bag Cards

Bag A **20 cubes** 8 blue 8 red 4 yellow	**Bag B** **8 cubes** 2 blue 2 red 4 yellow
Bag C **15 cubes** 15 blue 0 red 0 yellow	**Bag D** **10 cubes** 5 blue 0 red 5 yellow
Bag E **15 cubes** 3 blue 6 red 6 yellow	**Bag F** **12 cubes** 11 blue 1 red 0 yellow

Bag G	Bag H
10 cubes	**14 cubes**
1 blue	0 blue
3 red	8 red
6 yellow	6 yellow
Bag I	**Bag J**
12 cubes	**20 cubes**
5 blue	15 blue
4 red	1 red
3 yellow	4 yellow

Modeling Probabilities

I am a great proponent of valuing mistakes in the classroom. We know that when students struggle and make mistakes, they experience the greatest opportunities for brain growth (Boaler, 2016), and I have found in my teaching that when I tell students I want them to struggle and make mistakes, it is very liberating for them. Students spend much too much of their time worrying about being wrong, and students who do not know that mistakes are valuable often develop unproductive behavior, such as avoiding more challenging work and not persisting on mathematics problems. Everyone makes mistakes, and everyone struggles with mathematics, and we now know that this is really good for us all. It is so good for us, it makes me realize we should design our classrooms with more space for students to struggle and make mistakes. Many of us were trained with the expectation that students should be mostly correct in classrooms, as that would make them feel good and learn better. But the very best environment is one where we have encouraged struggle, given students really challenging material, and shared with them the value of struggle and mistakes. I share the value of mistakes and struggle by telling students about the brain growth that occurs (see Boaler, 2016, for more) and by sharing the famous mistakes made by mathematicians. I particularly like to share the famous mistake made by Andrew Wild in his solving of Fermat's Last Theorem, as it spawned a whole new area of mathematics.

When I discuss probability with students, I like to share a famous mistake made by the mathematician Jean-Baptiste le Rond d'Alembert, who was very famous in his time (the 1700s). A solution to wave equations is still often referred to as d'Alembert's equation. When d'Alembert was exploring probabilities, he reasoned that there were three possibilities that could come from throwing two coins: two heads, two tails and a head and a tail, and that the probability of each would be one third. This was incorrect, as there are two ways of throwing a head and a tail, giving four possibilities in total, and the probability of each outcome is one quarter. You may like to share d'Alembert's famous mistake with your students as you begin this set of activities, especially as these activities center around the act of calculating probabilities.

In these activities, we give students opportunities to work out simple and compound probabilities, and we introduce them to tree diagrams. A tree diagram is a really helpful way of visualizing probabilities.

In our Visualize activity, students find and compare the theoretical and experimental probabilities for tossing a cube onto different colored regions of a painting, connecting probability to area. We designed the activity to give students an opportunity to be physically active and to see that area can be used as a measure of probability if the units are found.

In our Play activity, students are invited to consider different dice games and the ways the design of the games changes the probabilistic outcomes available.

Our Investigate activity introduces students to an interesting probability manipulative called a Galton Board. These are boards that enable balls or other objects to fall through the board; with enough objects, it will produce what approximates a normal distribution, which can be seen visually. As the objects fall through the board, they can go to the left or the right, so the fall of the objects also presents opportunities to think about compound probabilities. These are the probabilities that arise when two independent events occur. In this instance, the probabilities are independent because the ball moves to the left or the right unaffected by whether it moved to the left or the right earlier. Usually Galton Boards are inflexible, and students just watch the balls or other objects fall through them, but in our activity, students make their own Galton Boards; they can also adapt the board design and see what happens when they do. Students can design, test, and model the probabilities on their different Galton Boards, with a different shape or height than those investigated by the class, and then compare their findings with one another.

Jo Boaler

Reference

Boaler, Jo. (2016). *Mathematical mindsets: Unleashing students' potential through creative math, inspiring messages, and innovative teaching.* San Francisco, CA: Jossey-Bass.

What's the Chance of That?

Snapshot

Students find and compare the theoretical and experimental probabilities for tossing a cube onto different colored regions of a painting, connecting probability to area.

Connection to CCSS
7.SP.7, 7.SP.6, 7.SP.5

Agenda

Activity	Time	Description/Prompt	Materials
Launch	10 min	Show students the What's the Chance of That? image and ask, If I were to toss a bead onto this image, which color would it be most (and least) likely to land on? Why? Make connections between area and probability.	What's the Chance of That? sheet, to display
Explore	30+ min	Groups explore the probability of a cube landing on each color of the What's the Chance of That? painting by analyzing the painting and conducting experiments. Students develop ways of finding and expressing probability. Groups compare their experimental and theoretical probabilities.	• What's the Chance of That? sheet (full color or wireframe), one per group • Centimeter cube or other small object for tossing, one per group • Books or other objects for forming a border around the image, for each group • Optional: colors

Activity	Time	Description/Prompt	Materials
Discuss	15+ min	Discuss the probability of a cube landing on each color and the methods students developed for finding these probabilities. Distinguish between theoretical and experimental methods and compare the results of the two types of strategies. Make connections between equivalent representations of probability, and connect probability to area.	What's the Chance of That? sheet, to display
Extend	30+ min	Groups design their own paintings for playing this tossing game. Challenge students to design a painting not based on 100 squares. Groups then find the probability of a cube landing on each color.	1″ grid paper (see appendix), scissors, colors, and tape, for each group

To the Teacher

This activity is designed to support students in connecting percents, fractions, probability, and area. In Big Idea 5, we introduced probability with spinners to build intuition and later moved toward quantifying probability with bags of countable cubes. Here, we integrate the ideas that area can be a measure of probability and that area can be countable if regions are decomposed into equal-size units. The painting we have adapted for students to explore is based on an underlying—and invisible—10 × 10 grid composed of 100 equal-size square units. The structure of this painting is similar to the one students explored when building ideas about percents in Big Idea 4, so students should have some experience with decomposing to quantify the portion each color represents. One reason connecting area to probability is particularly powerful is that area can serve as a model for probability. Even when area does not determine probability, as it does with a spinner, area can be used as a way of modeling probability, particularly for compound events. This is not the focus of this activity, but we are planting the seed of this idea here.

In preparing for this activity, you'll want to try experimenting with tossing a small object onto the painting to determine what students will need to make this work in your space. Centimeter cubes, beads, or other tossing objects need to be small enough to fit in a square unit, though they may often land on the borders between regions. Support students in thinking about what they will do if their object doesn't land completely inside one color. Any consistent approach is fine. We recommend providing students with some books to construct walls around the painting to keep the tossed object from bouncing out. Test out how high these borders need to be with the object you are tossing.

Activity

Launch

Launch the activity by showing students the What's the Chance of That? image on the document camera. Tell students to imagine that this painting is a game board. Ask, If you tossed a bead onto this board, which color would be most likely for the bead to land on? Which color would be least likely? Why? Give students a chance to turn and talk to a partner. Discuss students' reasoning, and draw attention to thinking that focuses on the area of each color.

Pose the question, What are the chances of a centimeter cube landing on each color?

Explore

Provide each group with the What's the Chance of That? sheet, a centimeter cube or other small object, and objects (such as books) to form a border around the painting. You can provide students with either the full-color or wireframe version of the sheet; if you use the wireframe version, you'll want to continue to display the color version on the document camera as a reference and provide access to colors.

Students explore the following questions:

- What is the probability of the cube landing on each color?
- How do you know?
- What are the different ways you can find the probability?
- What ways can you come up with to express the probabilities you find?
- What is the relationship between the experimental and theoretical probabilities you found?

Encourage students to both experiment with tossing the cube and analyze the painting itself to find the probabilities of landing on each color. For testing out their ideas, show students how to use the books to make a box around the painting to keep the cube in when tossed. Students will need to develop a way for dealing with instances when the cube lands on a boundary between two colors.

Discuss

Show the What's the Chance of That? sheet on the document camera as a reference. You can use this to mark up the ways that students analyzed the painting. Discuss the following questions:

- What is the probability of a cube landing on each color? How do you know?
- What strategies did you develop for finding the probability? Which strategies were experimental? Which were theoretical?
- What different ways can you come up with to express the probabilities you find?
- What is the relationship between the experimental and theoretical probabilities you found?

Highlight the ways students express probability, including fractions, decimals, percents, and language, and make connections between equivalent forms. Draw attention to the ways that students can use area as a model for probability, and connect this to the thinking students did with spinners in the Visualize activity from Big Idea 5.

Extend

Invite groups to design their own painting for this kind of game and find the probabilities of a bead landing on each of the colors they used. Provide students with 1″ grid paper (see appendix), scissors, tape, colors, and a bead or other object for tossing. Challenge students to design a painting that does not have 100 squares as the underlying framework. They will need to use their understandings of fractions, decimals, and percents to help them reason about area and probability.

Look-Fors

- **Are students analyzing the painting?** Much of the focus of Big Idea 5 was on building intuition about probability through experimentation. However, we want students to see that analyzing the possible outcomes is a more reliable and accurate way of predicting the probability of an event. As you observe students trying to find the probability of the cube landing on each color, look for groups that might be only experimenting. Ask students questions to support their thinking about analysis, such as, How do you know your probabilities are accurate? Is there any way to be more precise? How do you know from looking at the painting that one outcome is more likely than another? Is there a way to say exactly how much more likely? How could you use the painting as a tool for finding the probability of landing on each color?

- **Are students connecting area to probability?** One of the features of the painting we have designed is that it rests on an underlying 10×10 grid, with 100 equal-size squares. The probability of landing on a color depends on how large the regions of each color are, and the 100 squares in this painting make that area countable. To do so, students will need to decompose the painting into squares they can see. As you observe students working, look for whether students are decomposing the colored regions into equal-size pieces to quantify their area and connect that to the probability of the cube landing in that space. Students will also need to compose the separate regions that are the same color to find the total probability of landing on a given color, not just the probability of landing on one section of the painting. You might ask, Which color is it more likely for the cube to land on? How do you know? If students can name that it is the size of the region, or the area, that matters, then you can ask, If the area tells you how likely it is, then how can the area help you find the probability?

- **Do students see the difference between theoretical and experimental probabilities?** We began discussing the difference between theoretical and experimental probabilities in Big Idea 5, and in this activity, we want students to explore both and compare them. When the class discusses their findings, be sure to draw attention to the differences in the experimental probabilities that different groups generated for the same color and ask why this variation exists. You might ask, Why did you all get different results? Does this mean we made mistakes? Similarly, you might ask questions about the consistency of the theoretical probabilities that students found (or, if groups found different answers, you might ask the same questions that you did about experimental probability), such as, Why in this case did you all get the same results? Why is this different from experimenting? You might also ask students why we might use each kind of probability. In this activity, experimenting can serve as a check for finding theoretical probability, but in some cases, it may be very difficult to find theoretical probability, and what happens in real life is simply easier to see, as when skill and chance are combined.

- **How are students expressing probability?** We pick up this thread from the Investigate activity from Big Idea 5 and have designed this activity to provide a different kind of context for quantifying theoretical probability. Students may use fractions, words, ratios, decimals, or percents to express probability, and the underlying structure of the painting allows students to navigate any of these forms without focusing on calculation. Ask students, Why are you choosing to use this form? How does it help you compare probabilities? All forms can be accurate, but fractions, words, or ratios that do not reference the same size of whole can be difficult to compare. If the fractions all use the same denominator, however, they can be just as easy to compare as decimals and percents. When discussing the probabilities, be sure to make connections between equivalent forms of the same probability and ask, Which forms do you think are easiest to compare? Why?

Reflect

How is area related to probability?

What's the Chance of That?

Based on Leon Polk Smith's *Accent Black* (1949)

What's the Chance of That? (Wireframe)

Based on Leon Polk Smith's *Accent Black* (1949)

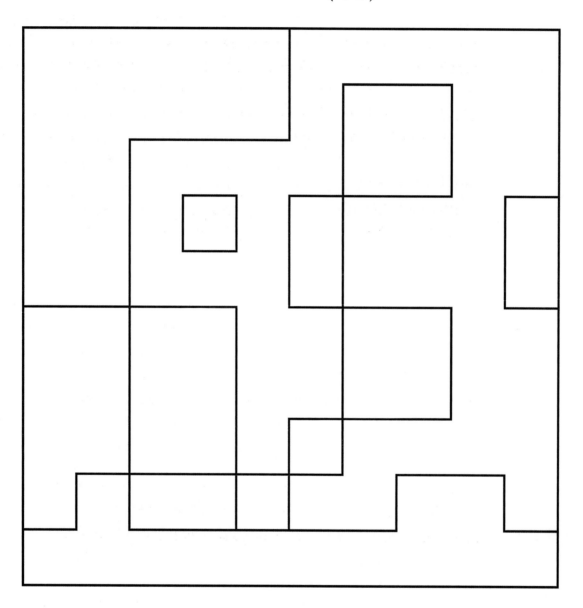

Probability Carnival

Snapshot

Students play multiple dice games to develop ways of modeling and visually proving the probabilities of winning and not winning.

Connection to CCSS
7.SP.7, 7.SP.6, 7.SP.5

Agenda

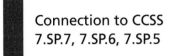

Activity	Time	Description/Prompt	Materials
Launch	5–10 min	Roll two dice on the document camera and remind students of how many games rely on this act. Tell students that there are many probabilities hidden inside dice. Describe how students will explore dice games and the probabilities of winning or not in a Probability Carnival.	Dice, two to display
Play	45+ min	Groups rotate among eight different dice game stations. At each station, students roll two dice, but determining the winner follows different rules. For each game, groups develop ways of modeling the probabilities of winning or not winning and construct a visual proof.	• Eight game stations around the classroom, each set up with two dice and a Probability Carnival Game Card • Make available: colors and grid paper (see appendix)

Activity	Time	Description/Prompt	Materials
Discuss	20–30 min	For each game, ask students to share their one-page visual proofs of the probability of winning or not winning. Come to agreement about these probabilities and then discuss what different models have to offer for finding or proving probability. Discuss what is happening in the rules of the games that lead to different probabilities of winning.	
Extend	45+ min	Groups develop their own dice games and model the probability of winning. Students share their games either by presenting them to the class or by swapping games with another group to play and to determine whether the game is fair.	• Dice, two or more per group • Make available: colors and grid paper (see appendix)

To the Teacher

In this activity, we extend the exploration students engaged in during the Play activity in Big Idea 5, where students figured out that when rolling two dice, not all sums are equally likely. Here we have developed eight games all played with two dice that determine winning differently, from rolling a prime sum to rolling a product that is a multiple of 3. The push in this activity is to model the outcomes and use those models to determine the probabilities of winning and not winning. Students might make organized lists or diagrams of possible outcomes, or they could construct area models. Take advantage of the diversity of representations, even if they are initial attempts, to share and discuss how these models help students see the chances of winning and make them quantifiable.

Students are likely to move through the stations at different paces. It helps if you have more stations than groups to give students the flexibility to move from station to station when they are ready.

Activity

Launch

Launch the activity by showing students two dice on the document camera and rolling them for all to see. Tell students that many board games involve rolling two dice, and remind students of the work they did in the Play activity in Big Idea 5 exploring the probabilities of sums. Tell students that there are many probabilities hidden inside these dice, and today this is what they're going to explore in a Probability Carnival.

Describe how the Probability Carnival will work and what the expectations are for moving around the room.

Play

Set up each of the eight dice games shown on the Probability Carnival Game Cards at different stations around the classroom. Each station will need two dice and a game card. Partners or small groups will need blank paper, grid paper (see appendix), and colors.

The eight games each involve rolling two dice, but winning is determined differently. Tell students that the rule on the card describes how you win the game. In the eight games, you win if your two dice roll a/an

1. Odd sum
2. Odd product
3. Sum less than 7
4. Product less than 15
5. Product that is a multiple of 3
6. Sum that is a factor of 12 or 15
7. Sum that is a factor of 12 and 15
8. Sum that is prime

Groups visit each station (or as many as they have time for), and at each station students do the following:

- Explore the game.
- Develop a method for modeling the probability of winning and not winning this game. This might include gathering data, making lists, or drawing diagrams.

- Create a visual proof of the probability of winning or not winning on full sheets of blank or grid paper (see appendix). Use color, drawing, symbols, numbers, labels, or words to communicate the model they made of the probability of winning and not winning. Encourage students to be creative and convincing.
- Keep working at a station for as long as it is useful, and then move on to another station.

Discuss

For each game, discuss the different visual proofs students have developed and the ways they expressed the probabilities of winning and not winning. If students don't agree on the probabilities, spend time exploring students' different ideas and come to agreement on the models that convince the class.

Discuss these questions:

- How did you find the theoretical probability of winning?
- What visual proofs or models are useful for seeing how likely it is to win?
- What did you need to show to prove the probability of winning?
- In which game is a player most likely to win? Least likely to win? Why?
- What is happening inside the game that shifts the probability of winning?

Draw students' attention to the different models they constructed, including any use of pictures, diagrams, area models, lists of outcomes, or other tools for analysis of theoretical probability. Expect that students will invent diverse ways of finding and showing probability, and use the discussion to highlight what each method has to offer as a tool.

Extend

Invite students to extend their exploration of modeling probabilities with dice games by creating their own games. Students might do the following:

- Continue to use two dice and develop different rules than those in the games in the Probability Carnival.
- Explore the same rules from one of the Probability Carnival Game Cards, but with three dice.

- Develop a game with different kinds of dice, such as 20-sided dice or dice with different numbers.

Students model and experiment with the probabilities of winning and not winning the games they devise. Invite students to share the games they have created and how they have modeled the probability of winning. If multiple groups create different games, they can exchange games to play and to determine whether the game is fair or not.

Look-Fors

- **Are students interpreting the rules accurately?** The rules for these games rely on students having some fluency with properties of numbers, such as *even* and *odd, primes, factors,* and *multiples.* Students also need to attend to when the two dice should be added or multiplied. These rules create two steps: performing an operation and then checking the result against the criterion for winning. If students do not accurately interpret both of these steps, they will be analyzing a different game. If students seem unfamiliar with (or seem to be misinterpreting) the concepts being used in the rule, take time to slow down the game play and ask questions about what these ideas mean. This could be a moment where telling is productive. For instance, you might explain what *multiple* means and then support students in identifying instances where the product is and isn't a multiple of 3.

- **Are students generating the possible outcomes of the game?** The only way to determine the proportions of instances where the player can win is to analyze the possible outcomes of rolling. In the games we've designed, students will either have to add or multiply the values of the two dice, which generates two alternative sets of outcomes. Look for whether students are creating an organized map of these outcomes that they can analyze against the rules of the game. Students need to consider that rolling a 6 and a 1 is a different outcome from rolling a 1 and a 6, which may not be apparent without a systematic way of generating all the possible outcomes. Tables (or area models), tree diagrams, and lists can all be used effectively for this purpose. You might ask, How will you know that you've found all the possible outcomes? How can you be sure you haven't missed one?

- **How are students connecting outcomes and models to probability?**
Beyond determining the possible outcomes and creating models of the game, students will then need to determine how these ideas connect to probability. It is not enough in these games to know whether the game is fair or not. We want students to quantify the probability. In each case, there are 36 possible outcomes, some that win and others that lose. You might ask, How will you use your model (or these possible outcomes) to figure out *how* likely it is to win the game? It makes sense to describe these probabilities as fractions or ratios, such as 14 out of 36, because these will still be comparable, but students may want to use percents. In either case, the goal is to move from the model to a precise expression of probability.

Reflect

Why are some dice games fair and some not?

Probability Carnival Game Cards

Game 1

- Roll two dice

- You win if the sum of the dice is odd

Game 2

- Roll two dice

- You win if the product of the dice is odd

Game 3

- Roll two dice

- You win if the sum of the dice is less than 7

Game 4

- Roll two dice

- You win if the product of the dice is less than 15

Game 5

- Roll two dice

- You win if the product of the dice is a multiple of 3

Game 6

- Roll two dice

- You win if the sum of the dice is a factor of 12 or 15

Game 7

- Roll two dice

- You win if the sum of the dice is a factor of 12 and 15

Game 8

- Roll two dice

- You win if the sum of the dice is a prime number

Go, Go Galton Board!

Snapshot

Students investigate compound probability by using geoboards to make Galton Boards, random sorting machines.

	Connection to CCSS
	7.SP.7, 7.SP.8, 7.SP.6, 7.SP.5

Agenda

Activity	Time	Description/Prompt	Materials
Launch	10 min	Show students a Galton Board you have constructed and ask them to watch closely as you drop a dime in. Discuss what happened to the dime. Define the end points as *outcomes* and show the number of levels on the board that the dime moved through.	Galton Board, constructed out of an isometric geoboard, rubber bands, and a dime, to demonstrate
Explore	40+ min	Groups construct their own Galton Boards, beginning with one level and increasing in size. They investigate the probabilities of each outcome in the different-size boards and create models for these probabilities.	• Isometric geoboard, rubber bands of various sizes, and a dime, for each group • Isometric dot paper (see appendix), for each group • Make available: colors
Discuss	20 min	Discuss the models students have created for the probabilities of each outcome in different-size boards. Discuss what the probabilities are, whether each outcome is equally likely, and why that might be. Name these events, when the board has two or more levels, as *compound probabilities*.	
Extend	30+ min	Groups design, test, and model the probabilities on their own Galton Boards, with a different shape or height than those investigated by the class. Students compare their findings to the patterns the class noted with the Galton Boards they investigated earlier.	• Isometric geoboard, rubber bands of various sizes, and a dime, for each group • Isometric dot paper (see appendix), for each group • Make available: colors

To the Teacher

This investigation involves a sorting machine called a Galton Board, in which a ball is dropped onto a series of pins, bouncing off the pins as it falls. Each time the ball hits a pin, it bounces either left or right. Through a series of these left-or-right chance events, the ball eventually falls in one of many final positions at the bottom, or outcomes. The taller the Galton Board, the more pins it includes and the more outcomes that are possible. The Galton Board, also known as a quincunx machine or bean machine, was invented by Sir Francis Galton in the late 19th century to model the normal distribution. When a large number of balls are dropped into a Galton Board, the balls fall most frequently in the center-most outcomes, known as a normal distribution, with the frequency tapering toward the outer outcomes, as shown in Figure 6.1.

Figure 6.1 On a Galton Board, the balls fall through the board, changing direction when they hit each pin. The more balls that fall through the board, the more closely the results model a normal distribution.

Source: Shutterstock.com/Peter Hermes Furian

We invite students to explore compound probabilities using Galton Boards of increasing height. If the board has only one pin (or level), then there are two outcomes, left or right, which are equally likely. We ask students to explore what happens when these boards have two, three, four, or more levels.

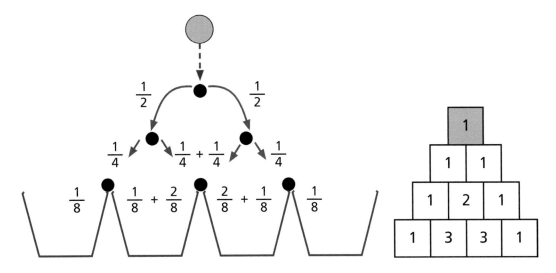

This image shows three levels. At the first pin under the green ball, the outcome is left or right, and each has an equal chance of $\frac{1}{2}$. At the next level, the ball may go left-left, left-right, right-left, or right-right with equal chance. The outcome of the outside paths (left-left or right-right) will each occur on average 1 in 4 times; the center path will occur on average 2 in 4 times as the ball falls left-right or right-left.

The outcomes for each level have an interesting connection to Pascal's Triangle.

For students to create their own Galton Boards for investigation, we have adapted isometric geoboards to create ever-growing and adaptable sorting machines. Large geoboards (11 × 11) with square and isometric arrangements on opposite sides are available, and you will need only one board per group. We've found that Galton Boards can be created using rubber bands or pipe cleaners of various sizes, and instead of a ball, a dime or washer works well. To make boards, you'll want to keep the rubber bands or pipe cleaners on the outside of the pins, as shown in Figure 6.2.

We encourage you to test your Galton Board before doing this activity with students. One factor is the angle of the board when you drop in the dime. You'll want to prop it up on a stack of books or bins, rather than try to balance it vertically, which will cause the dime to fall out. Try out the angle so that you'll be able to demonstrate how Galton Boards work for the class and support students in constructing their own. In our example, we found an angle between 10° and 15° worked well.

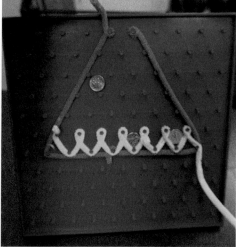

Figure 6.2 Here we have constructed a Galton Board using pipe cleaners. The board has five levels. In the image on the right, the dime is traveling down the outside path. Two other dimes have landed in the output areas.

Activity

Launch

Launch the activity by showing students a Galton Board with at least four levels made on an isometric geoboard. Ask students to watch closely, then drop a dime into the Galton Board. Ask, What happened? Give students a chance to turn and talk to a partner, and then take some of their observations. Be sure students see how the bouncing creates different outcomes at each level, and that the dime's moving left or right at each pin is equally likely. You may want to show a dime falling through the board more than once.

Name the slot the dime falls into at the end as the *outcome* of the Galton Board, and show students how many outcomes your board has. Point out the levels in the board you've just shared. Each level has a row of pins that the dime can bounce off of. Tell students that Galton Boards can come in all different sizes with different numbers of levels, and today they will be investigating the outcomes of boards with one, two, three, four, and more levels.

Tree diagrams are useful models for understanding compound events. You may choose to share with students a basic tree diagram before engaging with the Galton Board. For example, a tree diagram for flipping a fair coin three times would look

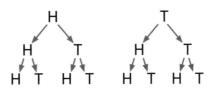

First toss
Second toss
Third toss

Figure 6.3

like Figure 6.3. Alternatively, you might look for opportunities to share this way of modeling probabilities with groups during the exploration, when students are grappling with how to capture the pathways on paper.

You may want to choose to share a basic tree diagram for the Galton Board. An important difference is the path where a ball can end in the same outcome from two different directions. In the previous diagram, you can see the sum of two fractions representing this possibility.

Explore

Provide each small group with an isometric geoboard, a set of rubber bands (including some large bands), a dime, and isometric dot paper (see appendix). Make colors available. Each group explores the following questions:

- On a Galton Board, is each outcome equally likely?
- How can you model the probability of each outcome?
- What is the probability of each outcome as the Galton Board gets larger?

Groups begin by making and testing a Galton Board with one row and two outcomes, and modeling what is happening. Encourage groups to make, test, and model Galton Boards with 2, 3, 4, or more rows to investigate what happens to the probability of the outcomes as the board grows. Groups can use the isometric dot paper (see appendix) to record results, draw their boards, or model the outcomes.

Discuss

The goal of the discussion is to focus on how students modeled the probabilities of the outcomes. Testing and seeing how the coin moved through the machine can help students visualize the action of the Galton Board, but to find probability with precision, a model is needed. For this, students needed to focus on the possible outcomes and how they are reached by the coin. Gather students together and discuss the following questions:

- What models did you create to help you understand how Galton Boards work?
- How do our different models compare? What do they have in common? What do they enable us to see?
- How did you use your models to think about the probability of different outcomes for the Galton Boards? (Discuss each size of machine from one row [two outcomes] through four rows [five outcomes] or more.)
- How did your models change as your Galton Board got larger? Why?
- On a Galton Board, is each outcome equally likely? Why or why not?
- If you were to put 100 coins through a large Galton Board, where would you expect the coins to fall? Why?

Name for students that what they have been exploring are called *compound probabilities,* or the probability of two or more events happening together. On the Galton Board, the compound probabilities involve the dime moving first in one direction (bouncing at the first level, left or right), and then in another direction (bouncing at the second level, left or right), and so on until it lands in the final outcome.

Extend

Invite groups to design and test their own Galton Boards with a different shape or height and create a model of the probabilities involved. Groups investigate the following questions:

- What are the probabilities of each outcome on your board?
- How does your board compare to the Galton Boards we tested as a class?
- How do the probabilities compare to the Galton Boards we tested as a class? Why might they be similar or different?

Look-Fors

- **Are students constructing Galton Boards that enable them to test probability?** Putting together a functioning Galton Board using an isometric geoboard, rubber bands, and a dime takes care. We've found that the position of the rubber bands matters, as they can narrow the passageways for the dime so much that the dime can get stuck on its way down. The angle of the boards matters also; if it is too steep, the dime flies out, and if it is too shallow, the dime won't bounce all the way down. To construct a working board, students will need some large rubber bands, which often come with geoboards, that can stretch around the perimeter of the Galton Board. Without a functioning Galton Board, students will become frustrated and unable to investigate the phenomenon in action. Support students in troubleshooting their Galton Boards before they start the work of modeling the outcomes so they can test what is happening.

- **Are students thinking about probability as compounding?** For students to model what is happening with the dime as it moves through the Galton Board, they need to interpret each level as a new event, in which the dime will move left or right. For instance, when the board has two levels, students need to be considering each outcome as being the result of two events, one at the first level and then a separate event at the second level. It can be useful for students to model the dime moving through each point where a choice is made, starting with a small Galton Board. If students are struggling to think of the events as compounding, you might ask, What could have happened to the dime when you dropped it in? What are the different pathways it could have followed? How do you know when you've found all the pathways that are possible? Are the pathways equally likely? Are the outcomes equally likely? Distinguishing between the pathways the dime could follow and the outcomes at the end will help students begin to model probability.

- **How are students making models of the probabilities in the Galton Board?** The key to modeling the probabilities of each outcome in a Galton Board with two or more levels is to think about the pathways that the dime could follow. Models of the probabilities will represent those pathways and how they accumulate into outcomes, as many of the outcomes can be achieved by more than one pathway. Students might model these by diagramming the different pathways of the Galton Board on isometric dot paper (see appendix), using arrows, lines, or colors to show how the outcomes are achieved. Students might also use an area model to show that at each level, there are an increasing number of binary decisions being made. Students can also model these outcomes mathematically, using numbers and symbols. If students choose this kind of model, be sure to ask probing questions to ensure that they can connect it back to what is happening with the Galton Board. As students grow their boards, they may begin to see patterns that change the models they select. You might ask, Why did you change your model? Why do you think this model is more useful than the last? Be sure to discuss these evolving models in the discussion and compare different types of models used across the class.

Reflect

What models for finding compound probabilities do you think were most useful? Why?

BIG IDEA **7**

Sampling to Understand Populations

In this big idea, we take on a mathematical area that is critical for the world: sampling. When scientists want to know the population of the world at any given time or the number of great white sharks in the Atlantic Ocean, they cannot count every person or shark. Instead they use methods of sampling. The result people come up with after they sample is necessarily an estimate. I always think it is valuable for students to engage with estimates in mathematics. It is a good opportunity for them to know that mathematics is not always precise and that some of the most important uses of mathematics are based on estimates.

Statisticians consider there to be two types of sampling, which they describe as probability sampling and nonprobability sampling. With probability sampling, you start with a complete frame of people (or objects). For example, someone might be looking to represent a town using a sample, and collect names from the electoral records in a town, but such records often exclude homeless people, so the sample would not be completely representative. Probability sampling methods tend to be time consuming and expensive. In nonprobability sampling, you do not start with a complete sampling frame, so some individuals have no chance of being selected. This limits the generalizability of the sample. However, nonprobability sampling methods tend to be cheaper and more convenient, and they are very useful for exploratory research and hypothesis generation. Some nice questions to ask students include, What kind of sample do you have? Does it survey all of the population, or are there some groups that are not represented?

In our Visualize activity, we present some works of art for which there is no clear way to determine the number of beads or dots used in the artwork. Students are introduced to photo images and asked to make predictions by estimating the amount of each different color bead that would be needed to reproduce the artwork. Students are asked to come up with their own strategies and methods to estimate the color. We anticipate that students will determine their own ways of sampling and connect what they have learned about ratio and proportion to justify their predictions.

In our Play activity, students are introduced to the big idea of sampling to represent a population. They will consider some populations of objects that are too big to count. Often students are asked to approximate the number of gumballs, or other candies, in a jar, and the person who comes closest to guessing the correct amount wins a prize. In this activity, students will take a sample, mark their results, and replace the object so that they can sample again. We ask students to continue to sample, mark, and replace so that they can draw conclusions about the makeup of the population. Students will work to organize their data and report their methods and findings, just as scientists do as they work to determine a population.

In our Investigate activity, we provide images of wildlife populations and ask students to determine how many animals are represented. Unlike the art we used in the Visualize activity, these images do not have pattern or symmetry. These actual photos contain images of different animals with variations that enable students to decide how they will categorize and analyze the populations. This is a situation in which "catch and release" will not work, so students will need to think of new ways to determine population. At the end of the lesson, we ask students to summarize and analyze the different methods and populations they have experienced in this big idea.

Jo Boaler

Sampling Dots and Beads

Snapshot

Students invent ways of sampling to understand the representation of different color dots and beads in nonrepeating designs.

Connection to CCSS
7.SP.1, 7.RP.3

Agenda

Activity	Time	Description/Prompt	Materials
Launch	10–15 min	Show students the tile and beadwork designs and ask them to make observations. Discuss which colors students perceive as most and least common in the designs and how they came to those predictions. Tell them that to reproduce these patterns, large or small, they would need a way to estimate the portion each color represents.	Aboriginal Dot Painting sheet, to display
Explore	30+ min	Groups choose an image to explore first and then develop strategies for finding the proportion of the design each color represents.	• Aboriginal Dot Painting sheet, for each group • Huichol Beadwork Rhino sheet, for each group
Discuss	15–20 min	Discuss the strategies that groups developed for finding the proportion of a design each color represents. Compare the strategies that groups used and the results they produced. Focus on the ways that students simplified the task by looking at a portion of the design, and name this as *sampling* the *population* of tiles of beads.	

To the Teacher

In this activity, we open the door for students to invent sampling as a way to understand populations. While we typically think of populations as groups of living things, such as people or wildlife, a population can be any large, diverse group of related elements. Here we use two nonrepeating patterns, one made with dots and the other with beads, to encourage students to select only a part of the population to examine and then use that to extrapolate estimates about the population at large. In life, counting all the members of a population is often impossible, and sampling is the only way to gain statistical insight into the whole. As you observe students developing ways of thinking about the proportion of the design each color represents, look for how students simplify the task by isolating sections to count or measure. As students talk about these strategies in the discussion, name what they were doing as *sampling* and introduce the language of *population* to describe the design as a whole. We will continue to use and build on these ideas throughout this big idea.

Note that the Huichol beadwork rhino is much more challenging than the Aboriginal dot painting, which we use to introduce the activity. The rhino is a three-dimensional object, making the full design impossible to see. This image forces sampling because we do not have access to all the parts of the design, and students will need to extend the sampling methods they develop on the dot painting to draw conclusions about the proportion of each color used to construct the rhino. Wait to provide groups with this image until you can see that they have developed methods for sampling the colors of the dot painting. The rhino image could, alternatively, serve as an extension for the whole class after the discussion.

Activity

Launch

Launch the activity by showing students the Aboriginal Dot Painting sheet on the document camera, and tell them that it is made up of dots on a dark brown surface. Ask students, What do you notice about this design? Give students a chance to turn and talk to a partner, then take some observations. Students may notice the detail or intricacy of the design, or the ways in which shapes and forms flow irregularly across the surface.

Aboriginal Dot Painting
Source: Shutterstock.com/shutterstock_97183103.jpg

Tell students to imagine that they are going to use this pattern to make this design out of dots, beads, or buttons. Drawing on what students have noticed, tell them that this design is so complex that we can't (and don't want to) count all these dots to know how many we might need of each color. Instead, we would want a way of figuring out approximately how much of each color we need.

Tell students that there are eight colors (dark brown, light brown, black, white, dark red, bright red, dark blue, bright blue) and that there are three more large dots (beige, red, and blue). Ask students, Based on what you can see, which color do you think is most common? Second most common? Least common? Could you order them from greatest to least in this design? Give students a chance to turn and talk, then ask not just for their answers but how they were formulating their predictions. Ask, What were you relying on to determine what was most or least common? Discuss the ways students were thinking about the prevalence of each color.

Tell students that today they are going to work with this pattern and develop more precise ways of estimating the portion of the design that each color represents.

Explore

Provide groups with copies of the Aboriginal Dot Painting sheet. Students develop strategies to address the question, What portion of the design does each color represent?

Be sure students understand that the goal is not to get a count of the dots but to gain a sense of their proportions. For instance, are the light brown dots half of the design? Or $\frac{1}{3}$? Or $\frac{1}{4}$? Or 20%?

Groups should work on the Aboriginal Dot Painting sheet for as long as it is useful, and then invite students to try their strategies out with a more challenging image, the Huichol beadwork rhino. Provide groups with the Huichol Beadwork Rhino sheet as they are ready, and point out that this sculpture is made up of beads. Ask students to explore the same question, What portion of the design does each color represent? Ask students, Will you be able to use the same strategy, or will you need to try something new?

Discuss

Invite students to share their strategies and observations on the document camera as you discuss the following questions:

- What strategies did you develop for understanding the relationship between the colors in each design?
- How are the strategies we used similar or different?
- (Draw attention to how students used smaller sections to make conclusions.) How did you choose your sections? Does it matter? Why or why not?
- What proportion does each color represent in the design? How do you know? (Be sure to encourage debate, and discuss how precise we might want to be.)

Name that when students used smaller sections to make conjectures about the entire design, what they were doing is called *sampling*. We can call the entire design the *population,* and sampling part of the population can help us understand the population as a whole.

Look-Fors

- **How are students simplifying the task?** Notice the ways students simplify the task by examining smaller samples of the design. This is a central goal of the activity. If you notice students attempting to count the entire design, ask questions to help students develop a more efficient strategy, such as, Do you need to count the entire design to figure out the portion that each color represents? If not, what could you focus on to get a good estimate? If students are focusing on a smaller section, ask them how they selected the region to represent the whole design. You might ask, How did you choose this part to focus on? What makes you think that this part will tell you something about the whole design? Look for reasoned approaches to selecting a section, such as a repeating part of the pattern, or some section of a repeating part. If students just select without considering representativeness, they may not be able to make valid inferences about the entire design. For instance, if students were to focus on only the border of the tile pattern, they may not be able to draw conclusions about the central pattern.

- **Are students thinking about proportion?** In this activity, we care about the proportion of each design that the different colors represent, not the precise count of each color. A count of the beads or tiles of each color would become a materials list for making this pattern in exactly the size shown. Support students in thinking about how these patterns could be made very large or very small, so the exact count isn't a useful tool. Instead, what an artisan would want is a way of figuring out the count they needed no matter how big or small they wanted to make the design, and proportions are a useful tool for this. Ask, What portion of the design is black (or any color)? Is it half? 20%? $\frac{4}{10}$? How could you figure it out?

- **How precise are students being?** Precision is a mathematical practice, but determining the level of precision needed in a mathematical situation requires thinking though the purpose of the work. In this case, it would not be sufficient for our purposes for students to simply glance at the design and say that each color is less than half. We want a more precise answer than this, where the five or six proportions total to something close to one whole. However, students do not need to get bogged down in the difference between, for instance, $\frac{1}{8}$ and $\frac{1}{10}$ or 40% and 43%, because with a sampling strategy, we must expect a degree of error of several percent. As you observe students work, ask them how precise they think they need to be and how they are achieving that level of precision. Encourage students to check their levels of precision overall by assessing whether their estimates seem to work together to make approximately one whole.

Reflect

When might sampling be useful for understanding a population?

Aboriginal Dot Painting

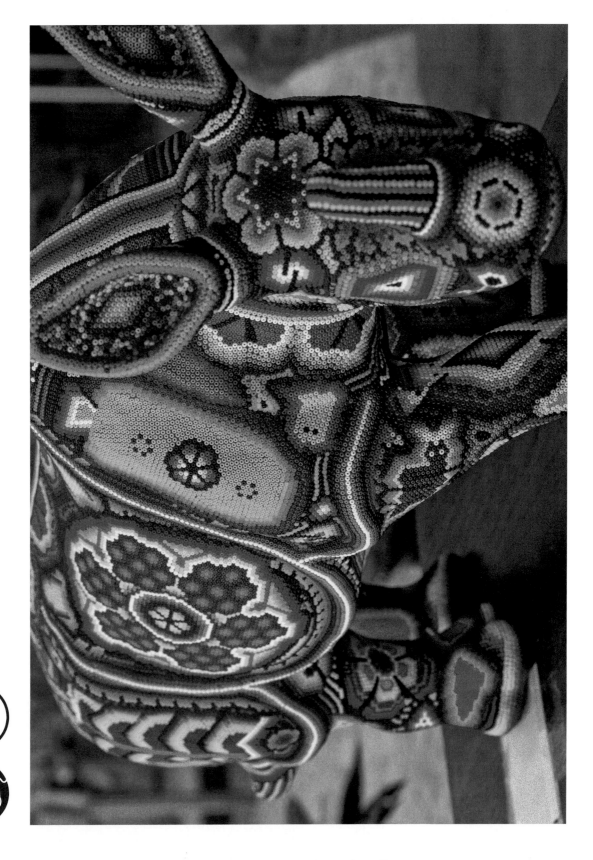

Huichol Beadwork Rhino

Catch and Release

Snapshot

Students use sampling to make inferences about the size and makeup of the populations of small objects, such as beads, beans, and buttons.

Connection to CCSS
7.SP.1, 7.SP.2, 7.RP.3

Agenda

Activity	Time	Description/Prompt	Materials
Launch	5 min	Show students one example of the populations they will work with in the activity, and point out the variation in this population. Tell students that their task is to figure out how to use sampling to draw conclusions about the makeup of the population as a whole.	Prepared populations of varied small objects (see To the Teacher section), to display and reference
Play	30 min	Using one population of objects, groups develop methods for drawing conclusions about the makeup of the population as a whole.	Prepared population of varied small objects, per group
Discuss	15–20 min	Discuss the methods that groups developed for using sampling to make inferences about the makeup of the population. Discuss how students decided how many samples to take and the size of those samples. Introduce the idea of "catch and release" to make estimates about the size, rather than makeup, of a population.	

Activity	Time	Description/Prompt	Materials
Play	20+ min	Groups develop ways of using sampling to estimate the size of the population through catch and release.	• Prepared population of varied small objects, per group • Permanent marker, one for each group • Make available: containers or scoops for sampling
Discuss	15–20 min	Discuss the methods students developed to use catch and release to estimate the size of their populations. Discuss how students sampled, how they used proportional reasoning to estimate the population size, and how they might increase the accuracy of their estimates.	
Extend	45+ min	If students are motivated to assess the accuracy of the population size estimates, invite students to count their populations and then compare these to the estimates. Discuss which sampling methods proved most accurate and why.	Prepared population of varied small objects, per group

To the Teacher

For this activity, you'll need to create collections, or what we will call *populations,* of objects that are too large to count and that have very clear differences within the population. You might use buckets, bins, or jars of dried beans, beads, sequins, buttons, or coins, which might include different colors or types. These differences need to be clear, not subtle, so that the objects are easy to categorize. You want a small number of categories of difference, approximately three to eight, and it will be particularly useful for this activity if the objects are not equally distributed across these categories. For instance, if there are four colors, sampling will be more interesting if these colors are not each $\frac{1}{4}$ of the whole; instead, one could represent close to $\frac{1}{2}$, and another might be close to $\frac{1}{8}$ or $\frac{1}{10}$ of the population, with the others in between.

When students move on to estimating the size of the population through catch and release, you will need to provide the groups with permanent markers to mark the sample they catch. If you have multiple classes using the same samples, we suggest you use different colored markers for each class so that they can distinguish between the marks they have made and those made by other groups of students earlier in the day.

Activity

Launch

Launch the activity by showing students one example of the *populations* they will be working with today. Point out that there are a huge number of objects in the container and that these objects vary. Be specific about the differences within the population. For instance, you might show on the document camera an example of red, yellow, green, blue, and purple beads. Show students the other populations they might explore.

Tell students that today their task is to figure out how to use sampling, as they did with the dot and bead designs in the Visualize activity, to draw conclusions about the makeup of the population as a whole. Pose the question, What can you learn about these populations by sampling?

Play

Provide each group with a container with a large population of objects (see the To the Teacher section). Groups explore the following questions:

- What different types or categories of objects exist in the population?
- What portion of the population is each category?
- How can you use sampling to make conclusions about the makeup of this population?
- What does it take to be confident in your conclusions about a population?

Groups test different ways of sampling and come up with a sampling plan that they feel accurately predicts the makeup of the population as a whole. Encourage students to test samples of different sizes and test different numbers of samples.

Discuss

Discuss the following questions:

- What conclusions did you come to about the population you studied?
- How did you sample to come to those conclusions? Why did you sample in this way?

- How did you decide how large a sample to take? How did you decide how many samples to take?
- What sampling methods might make our conclusions more accurate? What does it take to be confident in your conclusions about a population?

Be sure to discuss the impact of the number of samples students took and the size of those samples. Make connections to proportional reasoning, and talk about how students dealt with the variation in their different samples. For instance, if the first sample had $\frac{1}{3}$ red members but the next sample had $\frac{1}{4}$ red, how did students decide what proportion of the population was red?

Tell students that when scientists want to figure out the *size* (rather than the makeup) of a population of animals in the wild, one way they do it is to *catch and release*. Scientists capture some animals, tag them, and then release them back into the wild. Later they capture animals again and see what proportion are tagged and what proportion are not. How can this help us figure out the *size* of the population you have been exploring?

Play

Returning to the same populations, groups explore the following questions:

- About how big is the population?
- How could you use catch and release to estimate the size of the population?

Provide students with a permanent marker with which to mark the objects as they simulate catch and release. Make available some small containers or scoops that students can use for sampling. Encourage students to develop a plan for how to catch their objects and release them back into the population. Invite students to play with this method and develop ways of using it to estimate the size of the population.

Discuss

Note that it is a big stretch to think about catch and release and proportion, but we want students to have the chance to struggle with it. You may want to discuss what students have tried and noticed, and then send them back to continue work.

Discuss the following questions:

- How can you use catch and release to estimate the size of a population?
- What do you have to consider when you sample?

- What did you find when you released objects back into the population?
- What could you do to become more confident in your estimates?
- How big do you think your population is? Why?

In the discussion, be sure to highlight ways that students used proportional reasoning to estimate the size of the population they were studying.

Extend

If students are really curious about how close their estimate are, you can invite them to audit the populations by actually counting. The class can then use these counts to evaluate the accuracy of their sampling methods and discuss what made some methods more effective than others.

Look-Fors

- **Are students thinking about proportion when estimating population makeup?** Students can sample their populations many times and tally the members of each sample. This data can fuel larger conclusions about the population. When students sample repeatedly, they will likely record the number within each sample—for instance, that they scooped 26 beads, of which there were 6 red, 4 blue, 9 green, 5 purple, and 2 yellow. To make statistical inferences about the makeup of the larger population, however, students will need to shift at some point to thinking about the *proportion* rather than the *number* of each type of object. Look for how and when students are shifting to thinking proportionally. If students become stuck after sampling and recording, you might ask, What *part* or *portion* of the population do you think each color/type is? How could your data help you think about what fraction or percent each color/type is?

- **How are students reconciling multiple samples?** To estimate a population with accuracy requires either a single large sample or multiple smaller samples. If students use multiple small samples, they will have to think about how to address the differences in the samples they collect. If students shift to thinking proportionally about each sample, they will have different proportions for the different colors/types to reconcile. For instance, a group might find in four samples that red beads are $\frac{1}{3}$, $\frac{3}{10}$, $\frac{1}{4}$, and $\frac{2}{9}$ of each sample. Students might wonder, How do we deal with this variation? Some groups might want to offer ranges, such as, red beads are between $\frac{2}{9}$ and $\frac{1}{3}$ of the population.

Offering a range may be a more accurate and authentic way of estimating the population makeup. However, you'll also want to encourage students to make their best estimate of the overall population, even if they want to include a range, because this enables students to look across all of their estimates and see whether they make sense together (that is, if they sum to approximately 1). Ask, How can you use your data to find the most likely portion that each color/type represents? How could you put all of your data together to make an overall estimate? Students may find that it is easier to aggregate all of their counts first and then look at proportion.

- **How are students catching and releasing?** The mechanics of catching and releasing matter for the accuracy of the estimate. Students need to consider how their released samples recirculate in the population, as if they were wildlife, and deliberately mix the population thoroughly before sampling to count. If their tagged sample is very small, they will capture many samples that have no tagged members. Students need to think about such questions as, How many members should we tag? How big should our samples be? How many samples do we need to collect to make reasonable estimates? Ask the groups questions about these ideas to encourage them to make and try deliberate plans.

- **Are students using proportional reasoning to estimate population size?** Just as with the earlier sampling of population makeup, students need to apply proportional reasoning to estimate population size. However, now students need to attend to different members of the population (the tagged objects out of the sample) and use proportional reasoning to estimate the *number* of members of the whole population. To do this, students need to know exactly how many objects they tagged and then think about the proportion of those that show up in the samples they catch. For instance, if we marked 100 members of the population and they represent 5% of the samples we've caught, how many are in the whole population? Even posing this question is challenging, and students may struggle to formulate what they know and what they need to figure out. Encourage students to name what they know (or know how to find) and ask how they can use that to figure out how many objects are in their population. Expect struggle, and highlight insights that students have that might help the whole class move forward.

Reflect

How can sampling help you understand a population?

Wildlife Populations

Snapshot

Students investigate how to adapt sampling methods to estimate large wildlife populations from images.

	Connection to CCSS
	7.SP.1, 7.SP.2, 7.RP.3

Agenda

Activity	Time	Description/ Prompt	Materials
Launch	10 min	Show students the Antarctic Penguin Population image and ask them what they notice about the population. Connect this population to those that students have explored before. Ask students how they might use the methods they developed in previous activities to make conclusions about this penguin population.	Antarctic Penguin Population sheet, to display
Explore	45+ min	Groups select one of the six animal population sheets to begin their investigation. Groups adapt or develop sampling methods to make conclusions about the population shown, including the size of the population and its makeup. Students record evidence for their estimates. Groups look at multiple images to continue to investigate methods as the populations change.	Make available: animal population sheets and colors
Discuss	30+ min	Groups pair up with another that examined the same animal population. Groups compare their methods and results, and then discuss whether they could combine their approaches for a more accurate estimate. Repeat with another group pairing, if there is enough time. As a whole class, discuss the methods students used and what methods might be most accurate.	

To the Teacher

In this activity, we extend students' work on sampling to understand populations by examining a set of wildlife population images. Each image is of a large, difficult-to-count population with some sort of variation. Some populations include different species; others have different colors. The penguin image clearly shows adults and chicks. We ask students to investigate how they might adapt methods for sampling populations that they developed in the previous activities to draw conclusions about these images. Mathematically, these images present a different kind of challenge than the Aboriginal dot painting in the Visualize activity. There, students developed ways of sampling an image, but the dots were all visible and countable, if needed. The work students will do today is more similar to the Huichol beadwork rhino, where not all members are visible, though that image still represented a pattern with presumably symmetrical sides. The animal population images are not patterned, making selecting samples more challenging. As in the Play activity, we ask students to estimate the size of the population, but the catch-and-release strategies students used with objects aren't possible with static images. These populations are also more challenging to count, as the animals often overlap and may be very small. Students will need to develop some new ideas about how to sample to estimate population size with wildlife images.

Activity

Launch

Launch the activity by showing students the Antarctic Penguin Population sheet and telling them this image represents a population. Ask, What do you notice about this population? Give students a chance to turn and talk, and then collect some observations about the animals in the image. Students may notice that there appear to be two different kinds of penguins (adults and brown chicks) and that the animals in the distance are difficult to see. Make connections between this population and the objects they counted in the Play activity and the dots and beads in the Visualize activity. These are all instances in which the population is varied and too large to reasonably count.

Ask students, How can you use the different methods we've developed (or new methods) to make estimates about the wildlife in this location? Invite students to share some ideas about what they might do. You may want to record these ideas as a reference for the investigation. These ideas do not need to be well developed, correct, or detailed. Rather, they can be starting points. Tell students that today they will be investigating how to adapt the methods they have used before—or create new ones—to draw conclusions about wildlife populations in different images.

Explore

Make available the animal population sheets for groups to choose from and colors for marking up the images as needed. Small groups explore the following questions:

- How can you use the different methods we've developed (or new methods) to make estimates about the wildlife in these locations?
- How big do you think the population is?
- What is the makeup of the population shown?
- What conclusions can you draw? What questions do you still have?

Groups work on an image for as long as they feel that it is useful, and then try another. For each image, students record evidence of their strategies and estimates to share.

Discuss

Invite each group to find another group in the room that examined one of the images that they did. In these paired groups, ask students to share their methods and estimates. Then have the groups discuss the following questions:

- What did your approaches have in common? What made them different?
- How similar were your estimates?
- How could you use your methods together to come up with an even more accurate estimate?

If you have time, you might ask the groups to reshuffle by finding a different group to talk to about another one of the images. Repeat the discussion of methods the groups used.

As a whole class, discuss the following questions:

- What methods did you all use to make conclusions about the populations?
- How did you combine methods to come to a more accurate estimate?
- How did you all deal with variation in the population (for instance, when different kinds of butterflies were shown)?

If many groups looked at the same image, you may want to spend some time discussing the estimates and methods for that particular population. Be sure to discuss how students used sampling methods with these images when they could not draw random samples the way they did with objects in the Play activity.

Look-Fors

- **What sampling strategies are student using to account for the variation in these populations?** The populations in these images are different than those that students encountered in the two previous activities in this big idea. In the Visualize activity, students invented ways to sample populations that were countable and had some structure or organization. In the Play activity, the populations had no pattern but were likely evenly distributed, and they could be physically sampled and replaced. In these images, the populations have no structure or pattern, and they cannot be removed and counted as easily as beads in a bin. Catch and release is not a viable strategy. Variation in the populations may not be evenly distributed, with clusters of one type in some parts of the image. Furthermore, the populations may not be equally dense across the image, as with the penguin image, in which the birds in the foreground are larger and less dense than those in the background. Ask students how they plan to sample, and ask about the variation within the particular image students are investigating. Ask, How will you deal with this variation? If students have not attended to all the layers of variation in the image, point out places where you notice variation and ask students, How do you think this will affect your estimates? What could you do about that?

- **Are students thinking about both population size and makeup?** This investigation asks students to return to the dual estimates they made in the Play activity, of both population size and makeup. Notice whether groups are focused only on one type of estimate and be sure to ask questions about their sampling plans for both. Students may, very reasonably, have different sampling plans for making the two kinds of estimates. Ask, Why are your plans for sampling different (or, alternatively, the same)? Why might it make sense to have two different ways of sampling? Pay attention to how students are considering the different kinds of variation in the image in their sampling plans. Students may decide that they want to intentionally focus on one kind of estimate for multiple images so that they can compare how their strategy for estimating either population size or makeup works with different populations. This makes sense, and we encourage you to allow students to make these useful comparisons. However, remind students that they should eventually return to investigating methods for the other kind of estimate.

- **How are students using proportional reasoning to think about population makeup?** Drawing on the proportional reasoning that students used to sample their object populations in the Play activity, students should be well positioned to think proportionally about the makeup of these populations. We've intentionally selected populations that have some variation—in color, age, or species. Students will need to first identify in the image the variation that matters to them and then develop a sampling plan for addressing that variation. They need to consider, as discussed earlier, the ways that the variation may not be evenly distributed across the population or image. Because the variation is not evenly distributed, students may take several samples of the population and get very different results. Ask, How are you going to use such different results to make estimates about the whole image? How do you know your samples are representative? When you look at your estimates and compare them to the image, do they make sense to you? Why or why not?

- **Are students documenting their thinking in ways that others can understand?** Representing methods and evidence is key to making a convincing argument. Students will certainly arrive at different estimates than other groups investigating the same image; this is the nature of estimation. However, some estimates may vary widely, and in these cases it will be up to each group to provide support for their estimates. Even when estimates seem to agree across groups, comparing methods will enable students to understand the differences, find efficiencies, and develop ideas about what makes an accurate sampling plan. Students need to document their methods, using diagrams, pictures, numbers, words, and symbols to make clear how they sampled and how they used those samples to draw conclusions. The sharing structure we have recommended in the Discussion section will require each group to be able to share and justify their estimates to another group who investigated the same image; encourage students to view their documentation not just as visible work but as convincing evidence to share with another group later. You might ask, Would another person be able to look at what you've written and understand what you did? Is it clear? Is it convincing?

Reflect

When populations vary and are large, how can you use sampling to make accurate conclusions about the population?

Antarctic Penguin Population

 **Turkish Horse Population**

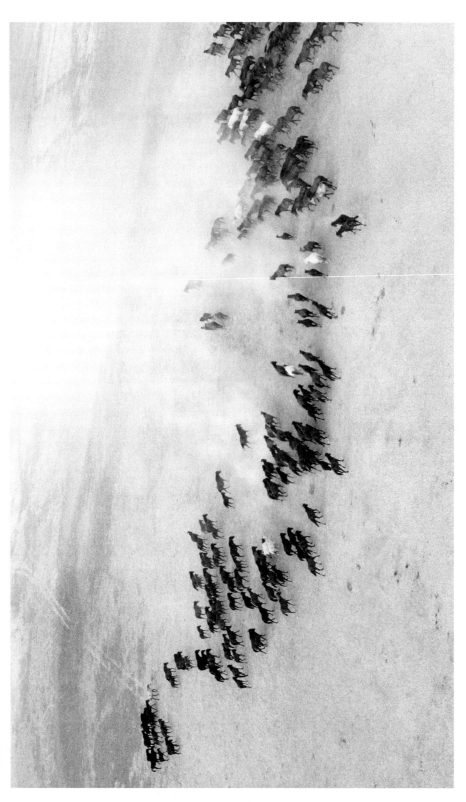

Mindset Mathematics, Grade 7, copyright © 2019 by Jo Boaler, Jen Munson, Cathy Williams. Reproduced by permission of John Wiley & Sons, Inc. *Source:* Shutterstock.com/fatir29

Butterfly Population I

Butterfly Population II

Mindset Mathematics, Grade 7, copyright © 2019 by Jo Boaler, Jen Munson, Cathy Williams. Reproduced by permission of John Wiley & Sons, Inc. *Source:* Shutterstock.com/Trahcus

194

Arctic Caribou Population

Operating with Opposites

Ask most people what mathematics is, and they will talk about numbers and operations. This is because of the overemphasis (in my view) on some parts of mathematics in the early years, and the underemphasis on other important parts. Numbers and operations make up a large part of the elementary curriculum, with too little time being spent on spatial thinking and reasoning. In addition (excuse the pun!), students are often taught to memorize math facts, instead of develop number sense and deal with numbers flexibly and creatively. I was at a conference of mathematicians recently when Francis Su, a mathematician at Harvey Mudd College and former president of the Mathematical Association of America, described memorizing the multiplication table as "one of the most meaningless activities possible." I agree with him! The common teaching of numbers and operations as rules to remember makes the particular set of activities in this big idea especially important. In this big idea, we give students a different way of seeing and interacting with numbers and operations, one that is visual, physical, and flexible, and probably quite different than anything they have experienced elsewhere.

I think of mathematics as a process of doing and undoing, because when students learn mathematical ideas, there is typically an opposite idea—or the undoing of the idea—that is also critical to learn and think about. This idea particularly comes into play in this set of activities.

In our Visualize activity, students will get the chance to move as a physical representation of the mathematical ideas of addition, subtraction, multiplication, and division. This will enable different brain areas to be activated and enable communication between areas of the brain as students relate their physical movement to numbers and operations expressed symbolically. The entire class will be invited to create a giant human number line. Each student will represent a point on the number line,

197

with approximately half the students representing consecutive positive integers, half representing consecutive negative integers, and one student on zero. Students will then move along the number line and visualize translations, reflections, dilations, and contractions.

In our Play activity, students will, again, experience numbers and operations differently, this time through play. The lesson provides an adaptation of a popular game of whole-number tic-tac-toe. In the activity, students will use integer game boards for addition and multiplication. Students work to get four or five in a row by covering a sum or product, depending on which game they are playing. The opposite operations of subtraction and division are also part of the game as students work to determine the addends or factors they need to achieve their desired sum or product in the game.

In our Investigate activity, students again receive an opportunity to encounter ideas differently. This time they are thinking visually about integer multiplication and division on a coordinate grid. We are excited about the possibilities of this lesson, as it enables students to think about and show multiplication as area. The lesson also provides opportunities for different thinking and different representations from students. For example, when we ask students to create a rectangle that has an area of –24, there are many different possible solutions. They will most likely begin by placing a vertex on the origin. Later they move all vertices into the quadrant and off the origin. They may even move the vertices to noninteger values, which would be exciting! What would it mean if rectangles cross over the axes? What does that do to their area? These are questions that students—and teachers—may wonder about and investigate together.

Jo Boaler

Line Dancing

Snapshot

Students create a human number line to physically represent what happens when we add, subtract, multiply, and divide with integers. Students can visualize the translations, reflections, dilations, and contractions these operations create.

Connection to CCSS
7.NS.1, 7.NS.2

Agenda

Activity	Time	Description/Prompt	Materials
Launch	5 min	Tell students that they are going to be exploring what it means to add, subtract, multiply, and divide with integers by making a human number line and moving.	
Explore and Discuss	45–60 min	Students positions themselves in two groups, one acting as integers on the number line and one acting as observers, flipping roles periodically. Through a series of prompts, ask students on the number line to move by adding, subtracting, multiplying, and dividing their number by positive and negative integers. Discuss what happens to the values on the number line as a whole and how these patterns of movement connect to the meaning of operations. Debate disagreements and mistakes. Create a class chart that records the patterns of movement that students observe and experience.	• Number line set up on the floor of a large space, with integers labeled from approximately −20 to +20 (see To the Teacher section) • Name tags, one per student, with their integer assignments on the tag • Chart and markers • Optional: video equipment for capturing the movement

Activity	Time	Description/Prompt	Materials
Extend	15–20 min	Students create their own integer operation problem, illustrate it, and discuss why the point on the line moved in the way the students have shown.	

To the Teacher

In this activity, we have borrowed a powerful idea for introducing integer operations physically that was developed by our colleague, researcher and teacher Jennifer L. Ruef (under review), which supports students in visualizing the patterns of movement created by integer addition, subtraction, multiplication, and division. Often we focus on looking at one example of an operation, such as making meaning of −2 + 3, but these individual cases can obscure the larger patterns that exist in integer operations. Rather than telling students what these patterns are and asking them to memorize, something that defies understanding and easily leads to forgetting, we want students to experience and develop intuition about these patterns so that they can make sense out of operations.

We use a structure for this activity that is different from any other in this book. Instead of sending students off to explore in partners or small groups, we use the entire class to enact a giant human number line. Each student will represent a point on the number line, with approximately half the students representing consecutive positive integers, half representing consecutive negative integers, and one student on zero. You will need a long space where you can set up a line with masking tape on the floor and spaces at equal intervals from approximately −20 to +20. A hallway, cafeteria, gym, or outdoor space could work. If you have the capacity, you could video what students do so that the class can watch it later as a reference. We recommend that during the work on the human number line, you have about half your class on the number line and half observing, and that students flip roles periodically. Some of the patterns that emerge are more easily seen from the observers' point of view, and this will give students the chance to both see and feel how operations affect integers. We recommend that you give each student a name tag with their assigned original number written on it. This will make it easier to reset the line to its original position.

During this activity, you will ask students on the number line to move in a particular way by performing an operation on the number they represent and moving to the resulting location. For instance, when the prompt is "Add 2," each student will consider their number and move to the new place that results when they add 2 to themselves; for example, the student standing on +4 will move to +6, and the student on −2 will move to 0. Note that we do not give students any direction in how to perform this movement, so students are going to make mistakes. These mistakes and any confusion are going to be obvious because they will not conform to the overall pattern. Use every mistake as an opportunity to talk with students about what makes sense and why. These are important meaning-making discussions and are at the heart of the activity, not a distraction from it. After each prompt, you'll discuss what happened and then reset the line by having students return to their original positions.

Several patterns can be seen when operating on the human number line. As you offer prompts that ask students to add and subtract from their values, students will see that what happens to the line is a shift, or *translation*. Everyone on the line slides to the left or the right the same number of units, so that all students are the same distance apart they were originally, just in a new location. Students can also see that subtracting a positive integer and adding a negative integer create the same movement; they are equivalent. These are crucial observations that help students connect what they know about operating with positive numbers to all integers.

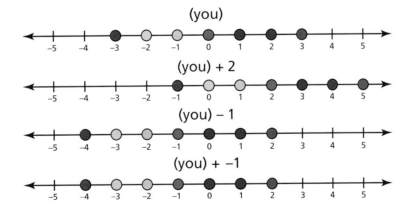

When students are asked to "Take the opposite" of their number, they will see that the entire line flips, or *reflects*. During this activity, we want students to see that taking the opposite is equivalent to multiplying by −1. This will enable students to see that they can decompose multiplying by −2 into two parts, multiplying by 2 and taking the opposite. When students multiply on the human number line, they will see a very different pattern than when adding and subtracting. Instead of the line sliding, it dilates. For instance, when multiplying by 2, the person at +4 will move to +8, and the person at –2 will move to –4. Students will all be in new positions (except 0), but they will no longer be one unit apart. Furthermore, students don't all move in the same direction; they bounce away from zero, with positive integers becoming larger and negative integers becoming smaller. The opposite occurs when dividing, with all numbers contracting in and becoming denser or closer to zero. As you move through the prompts, talk about what is happening, why, and what it means for the operation. Discuss what is happening to zero, who gets to move with addition and subtraction, but is stuck with multiplication and division.

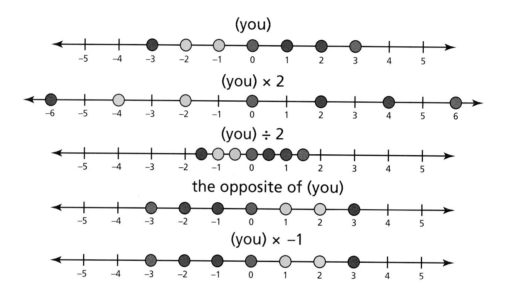

One goal of enacting this number line is to promote embodied cognition—that is, having a physical sense of knowledge in their bodies. As the class moves forward with integer operations, remind students of this work and how they and others moved when adding, subtracting, multiplying, and dividing. If possible, you may want to keep a number line on the floor in your classroom so that students can enact operations with their bodies when it is useful.

When you create the name tags for students, remember that you'll need two sets of the same integers. This way, when the observing group becomes the number line group, the line resets to the same starting position. For instance, if you have 26 students, you'll have a group of 13 students that begins the activity on the line representing integers from –6 to +6 and an observing group of 13 students who will also be wearing tags that include the numbers –6 to +6. When these two groups flip roles, the line will still look the same. Obviously, not all classes have an even number of students, but the line should look approximately balanced left to right and approximately the same when the two groups change roles.

Activity

Launch

Launch this activity by telling students that today they are going to explore the number line and what happens when we operate with integers—positive and negative numbers. Pose some questions to spark curiosity, such as, What does it mean to multiply by –2? What happens when we add –5? What does it mean to subtract –1? What happens to numbers when you divide by –3? Tell students that the best way to visualize what is happening when we add, subtract, multiply, and divide with integers is to make a number line out of ourselves and move.

Explore and Discuss

Direct students in how to arrange themselves. You'll want students to represent consecutive integers, with about half being negative and half positive, with someone on zero. We recommend that half your class be integers and half be observers. Tell students that they will flip roles periodically. Each student will need a name tag that indicates their assigned number. When a student's role is to observe, their job is to be able to communicate what is happening to the entire number line. When a student's role is to be on the number line, their job is to think about how to enact the operation on their number and see whether their ideas make sense with what others are doing.

For each of the following prompts, ask the students on the number line to move to what they believe is their new position. You may want to repeat each prompt a few times with different integers (such as adding a positive 1, 2, 3, and 5). If you change the numbers, be sure that your number line is long enough to accommodate the movement of all students. Be sure to periodically swap the students who are observing and on the number line so that students get both experiences.

Human Number Line Prompts

1. Add 2 (or any other positive integer) to your number and move to the new location.
2. Subtract 3 (or any other positive integer) from your number and move to the new location.

3. Take the opposite of your number and move to the new location.

4. Subtract –4 (or any other negative integer) from your number and move to the new location. (Note that this prompt will be confusing to students if they have never subtracted a negative number before.)

5. Multiply your number by 2 (or some other small whole number) and move to the new location.

6. Divide your number by 2 (or some other small whole number) and move to the new location.

7. Multiply your number by $\frac{1}{2}$ (or some other unit fraction) and move to the new location.

8. Multiply your number by –1 and move to the new location.

9. Multiply your number by –2 (or some other small negative integer) and move to the new location.

10. Divide your number by –2 (or some other small negative integer) and move to the new location.

After each prompt, discuss the following questions:

- Where did you move? Describe the movement of your individual point.
- How did the points on the number line change overall? (Observers will have the best perspective on this question.)

If there is disagreement about a point's movement, encourage debate to promote sense making by posing questions such as the following:

- What does this operation mean?
- Why might a particular movement make sense?
- How can we make sense out of the movement when we perform this operation?

For each prompt, add to a chart that has two columns for "When we . . .," in which you record the type of operation, and "The point on the number line moves by . . .," in which you record the type of movement observed. For each type of operation, use the discussion to add students' language to the chart to describe the movement, such as "When we . . . add a negative integer, the point on the number line . . . shifts to the left." Be sure to draw on language such as *shift, slide, flip, opposite, expand, dilate, stretch, shrink,* and *contract*.

Extend

Invite students to make up their own individual integer operation problem and illustrate what happens. For instance, students might create a problem such as -3×-8 or $20 - -16$ or $18 \div -6$. Partners work together to represent the movement on the number line and answer the question, Why does the point on the number line move in the way you've shown?

Look-Fors

- **Are there any students who seem to be parroting previously learned rules?** You will likely encounter students who have been taught in the past to memorize integer operation rules. You'll notice that these students will state the rule in a different way than those analyzing the movement on the number line. It might sound like, "When you multiply a positive and a negative, you get a negative." Listen for students parroting these kinds of rules, and push them to explain what it means and how it connects to what is happening on the number line. Students who have merely memorized a rule will struggle to make meaning out of it and may not be able to explain how this rule relates to the number line. Remind these students that the goal is to make sense of what is happening by observing the number line, making mistakes, and noticing overall patterns. Some students may be able to connect the rule to integer movement on the number line, and if so, ask them to share their thinking at the end of the discussion of the prompt, so that others have a chance to make sense of the movement on the number line before hearing the rule. You may also want to remind students that rules are easy to forget, but that they can always imagine what happens on the number line.

- **Are students making sense of mistakes?** For each movement, you will notice some students out of step or moving only by watching those around them. Capitalize on these opportunities to press the entire class to make sense out of the operation and the movement it creates on the number line. Ask, Why did it make sense to you to move there? Do we agree or disagree with this new position? Why? Each mistake offers students an opportunity to examine an idea that might appear to make sense, but ultimately does not. For instance, after adding and subtracting on the number line and observing the right and left shifts, some students might apply this pattern to multiplying, assuming that the same kind of movement makes sense. Use such a mistake to talk about why sliding won't work, and leverage students' understanding of positive whole numbers to make sense of integers.

- **Are students decomposing multiplying and dividing by a negative integer into a whole-number operation and taking the opposite?** One critical notion in this activity is that you can decompose integer operations by thinking about opposites. As discussed in the To the Teacher section, multiplying by –3 is equivalent to multiplying by +3 and taking the opposite (or vice versa). This decomposition is powerful because it means that students can leverage their deep understanding of operations with positive whole numbers to operate with integers. When this connection begins to surface, you may want to invite the class to test it by, for example, multiplying by –3 and seeing the result, and then multiplying by 3 and taking the opposite. Compare the results as many times as students need to confirm the equivalence of the two results.

Reflect

What surprised you the most when seeing the movement on the number line? What happened, and what does it mean?

Reference

Ruef, J. L. (under review). Human numberline: Embodying transformations. *Mathematics Teacher: Learning and Teaching PK–12.*

Integer Tic-Tac-Toe

Snapshot

Students play with integer operations through addition and multiplication tic-tac-toe games.

Connection to CCSS
7.NS.1, 7.NS.2

Agenda

Activity	Time	Description/Prompt	Materials
Launch	10–15 min	Show students how to play Addition Tic-Tac-Toe and model game play with the class. Press students to explain why the sum they found makes sense. Explain that Multiplication Tic-Tac-Toe is played the same way, but with products.	• Addition Tic-Tac-Toe game board, to display • Multiplication Tic-Tac-Toe game board, to display • Two paper clips • Objects for marking the board, such as chips or cubes in two colors
Play	20–40 min	Partners play Addition Tic-Tac-Toe and/or Multiplication Tic-Tac-Toe, making sure they agree with the squares each player claims. Students can use the number line to support their thinking.	• Addition Tic-Tac-Toe game board, one per partnership • Multiplication Tic-Tac-Toe game board, one per partnership • Two paper clips, per partnership • Objects for marking the board, such as chips or cubes, in two colors, for each partnership • Make available: Number Line sheets

Activity	Time	Description/Prompt	Materials
Discuss	15–20 min	Discuss the strategies that students developed for playing the games and how they connect back to what they understand about integer operations. Discuss how students decided how to move the paper clips and determined what space to mark on the board. Compare the strategies students used on the two different games.	
Extend	20–45 min	Partners design their own integer tic-tac-toe game boards and test their creations by playing. Partners may swap games with other groups to try new versions of the game.	Make available: Make Your Own Tic-Tac-Toe sheets, grid paper (see appendix), or rulers

To the Teacher

In this Play activity, we extend a common game used for building fluency with whole-number operations to include thinking about integer operations. Many students will have had experience with some mathematical form of tic-tac-toe, which should aid in explaining the rules. However, be clear about the specific ways these games work (including moving one paper clip at a time, and needing four in a row to win) so that students do not confuse the different versions they are likely to have played.

Our aim with these games is to build on the physical experience students had with the human number line in the Visualize activity to move students toward meaningful fluency with addition and multiplication with integers. Expect that students will struggle and benefit from returning to the number line as a place to model what is happening when they add or multiply with integers. We encourage you to continue to post the chart of integer operation patterns that you created with students in the Visualize activity as a resource for students to support sense making.

Activity

Launch

Launch the activity by showing students the Addition Tic-Tac-Toe game and explaining the rules. Play a couple of rounds of this game with the class in which you, the teacher, are Player A and the class, as a whole, is Player B. Ask questions about how students know what square to mark as their sum. Ensure that students understand the rules.

Show them the Multiplication Tic-Tac-Toe game and tell them that the rules are the same, but with multiplication. You may want to play a couple of rounds with the class for clarity.

Play

In partners, students play the Addition or Multiplication Tic-Tac-Toe game. You may want to invite students to play each game in turn so that they have experience with both. Provide each partnership with an Addition Tic-Tac-Toe game board and a Multiplication Tic-Tac-Toe game board, two paper clips, and colored objects, such as chips or cubes, for each player.

Rules for the Addition or Multiplication Tic-Tac-Toe Game

- Each player selects a number at the bottom of the board and places one paper clip on that number, so that two integers are marked
- Players take turns choosing and moving one of the two paper clips to any integer on the bottom of the board. They then mark the sum (in the Addition Game) or product (in the Multiplication Game) of the two numbers on the board using their object. If the appropriate sum or product appears more than once on the board, they must choose one square to mark as their own.
- The goal of the game is to get four in a row: horizontally, vertically, or diagonally. The first player to mark four in a row wins the game.

With each turn, both players must agree that the sum or product is marked accurately. If a student makes a mistake, their partner should convince them that this answer does not make sense and come to agreement on the correct sum or product. If students run into questions about what to do (for instance, what is -2×-4) and their partner has not been able help them make sense, pause the class and challenge students to reason through and model it together. Make available the Number Line sheets to help with visualizing operations and connecting reasoning to the Visualize activity.

Discuss

After students have had a chance to play for an extended time, discuss the following questions:

- What strategies did you develop for finding the sum (or product) of your two numbers?
- What strategies did you develop for choosing how to place your paper clip? What were you considering?
- When you wanted to get a particular number, how did you think about placing your paper clip?
- When you wanted to block your opponent, how did you have to think about placing your paper clip?
- How did your strategies have to change when you changed games?
- What patterns did you notice that helped you play the games?

Extend

Invite students to design their own game board for a different version of this game. Students may want to change the numbers that appear along the bottom or alter the operation to include subtraction. What would the game board look like? Would the rules need to be modified? If so, how? Provide students with access to the Make Your Own Tic-Tac-Toe sheet, grid paper (see appendix), or rulers to construct their boards. Groups design a new game and test it by playing several rounds. Partners may decide to revise the game based on their experience playing it to make it more or less challenging. Students may want to swap games with other groups to play these homegrown integer games.

Look-Fors

- **Are students reasoning or guessing?** Your students will be fluent with the positive integer operations represented on both game boards. In the case of multiplication, students will have to think most about whether the result is positive or negative. Even with addition, students may realize that they need to move a specific number of units either left or right on the number line. Listen for students who appear to be repeatedly guessing between two options, which might sound like, "16? –16?" or "–7? No, 1?" In this situation, spend some time supporting both partners in making sense of what movement is happening on the number line. If one partner appears to understand, support them in explaining or showing their thinking to the other. Provide these students with a copy of the Number Line sheet, and you may even want to have them stand up on a physical number line, if you have one in your room, to physically represent the movement, as they did in the Visualize activity.

- **Are students using the number line or class chart of operation patterns?** As you observe how students are working, you will no doubt be listening for answers that are accurate and for mistakes. But beyond whether students seem to be getting their answers correct, notice how they seem to be thinking through each move. Do you see students looking at or touching the number line? Are students writing on the number line or moving objects on it? Do students refer to the class chart you made during the Visualize activity as a guide for how to move, or do they seem to know what movement is needed? And, most important, how do students use these strategies differently as game play proceeds? You might notice, for instance, that for some types of problems, students use the number line less or not at all (for instance, with two positive integers or with adding two negatives) while they continue to use them in trickier cases (such as adding a positive and a negative or multiplying two negatives). If students appear to be consistently struggling, anchor their thinking back in the number line and the class's experience moving on it.

- **Are partners supporting each other in making sense?** There are several ways that partners might conceive of their role in this game. Partners might see this as a competitive experience and play gotcha with their partner's error, which would only penalize mistakes and undermine learning. Partners could, alternatively, take a passive role and not attend to where the other player is placing their markers, which would only allow misconceptions to take root. In the middle is an engaged role that notices and checks the placement of each marker and addresses any disagreements in a supportive way. This is not easy for adolescents, and you will need to explicitly support students in finding language for holding each other accountable to making sense, without ridicule or passive acceptance. Students might benefit from language such as, "I don't agree with where you've put your marker. Do you want to rethink it? Or do you want me to explain why I disagree?" Listen carefully for opportunities to shape the roles students play with each other and the talk moves they use to do it.

Reflect

How do these games help you think about subtraction or division?

Addition Tic-Tac-Toe

-9	1	8	0	2	3	9	6
-2	-3	1	-8	-1	10	-4	8
-10	4	-7	9	-6	3	-5	7
-9	-2	2	-3	0	-7	6	4
-6	-4	-1	5	3	-10	7	-2
2	0	-9	10	-5	8	4	-6
-7	-8	-4	-3	-1	-10	0	5
9	5	6	7	-8	-5	10	1

-5 -4 -3 -2 -1 0 1 2 3 4 5

Multiplication Tic-Tac-Toe

-4	-3	16	12	1	10	6	-16
15	20	-8	-6	0	-9	1	4
-20	-25	5	-12	-1	-25	-10	-9
-10	4	-15	-2	5	4	-12	0
12	8	16	6	9	20	-5	15
3	10	4	25	-4	-15	2	8
-5	0	-2	3	-12	-8	-20	3
-16	-4	15	-10	2	0	-6	-3

-5 -4 -3 -2 -1 0 1 2 3 4 5

Number Line

Mindset Mathematics, Grade 7, copyright © 2019 by Jo Boaler, Jen Munson, Cathy Williams.
Reproduced by permission of John Wiley & Sons, Inc.

Make Your Own Tic-Tac-Toe

Coordinating Multiplication

Snapshot

Students connect area to integer multiplication by examining patterns on the coordinate plane.

	Connection to CCSS
	7.NS.2

Agenda

Activity	Time	Description/Prompt	Materials
Launch	10 min	Show students the Coordinate Multiplication sheet and ask what it shows. Be sure students notice how the coordinate plane is showing the area of a rectangle and the product of two positive integers. Pose the question, How can we use the coordinate plane to show multiplication and division of both positive and negative integers?	Coordinate Multiplication sheet, to display
Explore	30–45 min	Partners investigate how they can represent integer multiplication and division on the coordinate plane and the patterns that emerge from this representation. Students can use the Problems to Explore sheet to launch their investigation and create their own to look for patterns.	• Coordinate Plane sheets, multiple per partnership • Colors, for each partnership • Problems to Explore sheet, one for each partnership • Make available: calculators and number lines (see Play activity)

Activity	Time	Description/Prompt	Materials
Discuss	15–20 min	Partners share the ways they represented integer multiplication and division on the coordinate plane and the patterns they observed. Discuss the different kinds of integers students explored and whether the patterns they observed changed or remained the same.	Coordinate Plane sheets, to display and for recording

To the Teacher

This activity builds on the connection between multiplication and area that students learned in later elementary school. The teaching of integer multiplication and division typically ignores the connection to arrays and area, despite the fact that building this connection with positive numbers supports students in making meaning of multiplication. We noticed that the coordinate plane can support visualizing how area connects to multiplication and division of integers, and this investigation centers on inviting students to explore this representation. The two axes of the coordinate plane provide four combinations of coordinates, just as there are four combinations of signed integers for multiplication: (positive, positive), (positive, negative), (negative, negative), and (negative, positive). Plotting a pair of coordinates as a point shows the point's position, but that position can be seen as the fourth corner of a rectangle with an area that is the product of the two coordinates. Our Coordinate Multiplication sheet shows this for two positive integers.

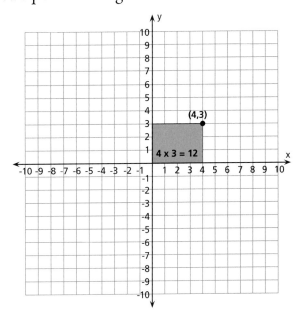

But what happens when we extend this into the other quadrants? We found an interesting pattern when plotting a group of problems in all four quadrants. The areas can all be counted on the coordinate plane; the positive areas occur in the first and third quadrants, while the negative areas occur in the second and fourth quadrants. These positive and negative areas correspond to lines with positive and negative slope. Another way of thinking about the positive and negative areas is that each time an area is reflected across an axis, we find its opposite. If we know that the area of a rectangle with positive side lengths is also positive, then reflection across each adjacent axis leads to a negative area, and reflecting that again to quadrant 3 returns the area to positive. These patterns of finding opposites connect to what students found on the human number line.

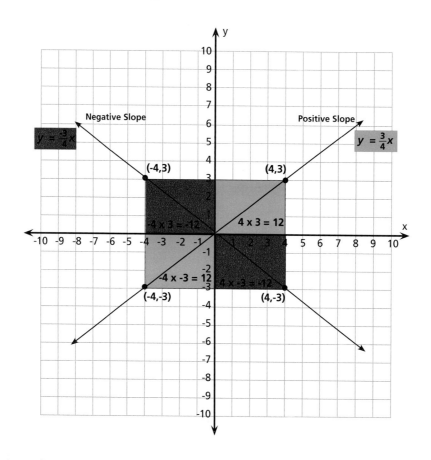

Extending this work to exploring division on the coordinate plane is challenging, as students need to consider what each number represents. In the problem $28 \div -4$, for instance, students need to interpret that one axis must have a point of -4 while the area of the rectangle will need to be $+28$. The patterns students observe when investigating multiplication should support students in deducing which quadrant this rectangle would be located in. Encourage students to focus on multiplication and its patterns first before trying to tackle division. We do not anticipate that students will ultimately want to use the coordinate plane as a tool for solving integer multiplication and division; rather, this investigation supports students in making connections to area and exploring patterns related to integer operations.

Activity

Launch

Launch the activity by showing students the Coordinate Multiplication sheet on the document camera. Ask students, What do you notice? What is being shown here? Invite students to turn and talk to a partner about their observations, and then collect their noticings. Be sure students notice how the coordinate plane is showing multiplication with positive integers.

Pose the question, How can we use the coordinate plane to show multiplication and division of both positive and negative integers?

Explore

Provide students with an ample supply of Coordinate Plane sheets, colors, and the Problems to Explore sheet. Make calculators and number lines available for students to support their investigation. Invite partners to explore the following questions:

- How can you use the coordinate plane to multiply or divide integers?
- What could multiplication and division of integers look like on the coordinate plane?
- Plot several multiplication problems on the coordinate plane. What are their areas? What patterns emerge when you multiply integers on the coordinate plane?
- Plot several division problems on the coordinate plane. What are their solutions? What patterns emerge when you divide integers on the coordinate place?

Students can use the Problems to Explore sheet to get their investigation started, but they do not need to restrict themselves to these problems. Students can invent their own problems to search for patterns.

Discuss

Discuss the following questions:

- How can you use the coordinate plane to multiply or divide integers?
- What could multiplication and division look like on the coordinate plane?

- What patterns emerge when you multiply or divide on the coordinate plane? How are they similar to or different from the patterns on our human number line? Why?
- How are the patterns similar or different when you change the numbers you explore?

Invite students to share their coordinate planes on the document camera to enable everyone to visualize the patterns students found when multiplying and dividing on the coordinate plane. You may also want to use copies of the Coordinate Plane sheet to collect patterns observed across the class.

Look-Fors

- **Are students connecting multiplication on the number line to multiplication on the coordinate plane?** As students plot the rectangles created on the coordinate plane, they will be able to see and count the areas, or the products. But it is not obvious from the coordinate plane whether the area is positive or negative. Students will need to use their understanding built on the number line to determine whether the area is positive or negative. Support students in thinking about what happened in the number line, and remind students that the coordinate plane is just two intersecting number lines. You might ask something like, "If you know that 6×3 is $+18$, then what does it mean to multiply 6 by -3?" Be sure to encourage students to color-code and label the rectangles they find in each quadrant so that they can begin to see patterns. In particular we want students to see that all products in the second and fourth quadrants are negative. Ask students to reason about this pattern as they work or in the discussion: Why are these always the opposite of what we find in quadrant 1 (or when multiplying two positive integers)?
- **Are students testing their ideas in problems they create?** We've supplied a set of problems to launch students' exploration with the idea that these could serve as models for students to extend. We specifically want students to compare the different combinations of positive and negative integers so that they can determine patterns that are visible on the coordinate plane. The problem types we've provided include sets of related multiplication problems, division problems, and those where the area is given but not the factors. Encourage students to use these as models for creating their own problems to explore, and to compare the results with what they found in

these examples. Ask, Are the patterns the same for all problems? What problems could you write to test these patterns and find out whether they are always or sometimes true?

- **Are students trying to tackle division before making sense of multiplication?** Multiplication is an entry point for considering division. Plotting multiplication on the coordinate plane will support students in finding patterns and making conjectures about the locations of positive and negative integers that they can extend to division. For instance, if students have found that areas in the second and fourth quadrants are always negative (and that the first and third quadrants always have positive areas), students will be able to use this pattern to determine where and how to locate a problem such as $-32 \div -8$ on the coordinate plane. If students launch into division before finding these multiplication patterns, they will find it difficult to determine how to plot this type of division problem. Students may be able to use the understanding they developed with the human number line to support them in making sense of integer multiplication and division. You might also ask students to think of division as a missing-factor problem, such as $-8 \times \_\_\_ = -32$. But it may be most productive to ask students to focus first on multiplication patterns and then use that to support visualization of division.

Reflect

How does integer multiplication on the coordinate plane relate to integer multiplication on the human number line?

 **Coordinate Multiplication**

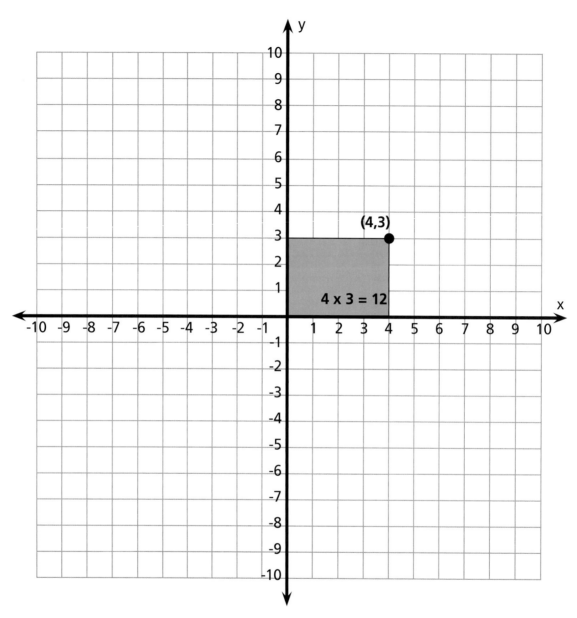

Coordinate Plane

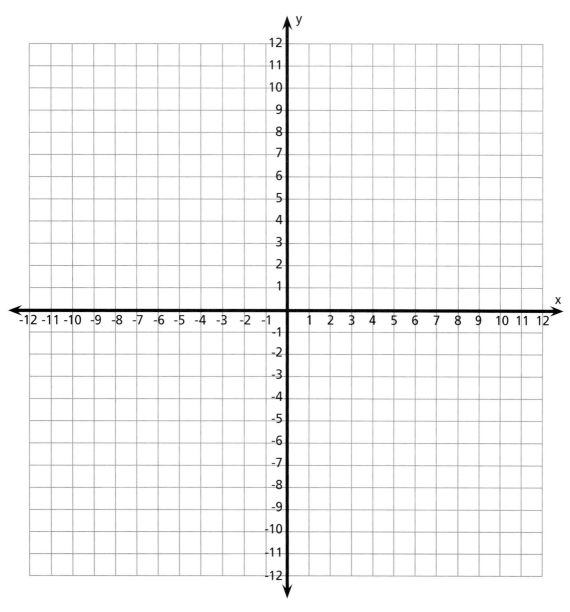

 **Problems to Explore**

Multiplication Problems to Explore	Division Problems to Explore
6 × 3	32 ÷ 8
–6 × 3	32 ÷ –8
6 × –3	–32 ÷ 8
–6 × –3	–32 ÷ –8
3 × 6	28 ÷ 4
–3 × 6	28 ÷ –4
3 × –6	–28 ÷ 4
–3 × –6	–28 ÷ –4
What rectangles can be made for an area of 24?	What rectangles can be made for an area of –24?

Using Algebra as a Problem-Solving Tool

Algebra is a central part of mathematics and of quantitative thinking more generally; symbolic and functional thinking is frequently used to solve problems. Algebra is, as we describe it in the big idea title, a problem-solving tool. Sadly, students who have been taught algebra with traditional methods do not describe it in this way, or appreciate the role of algebra in problem solving. Instead they see algebra as "something to solve for." This is due to the way they have been taught—not with interesting problems that algebra can help with but with repetitive exercises when they try to solve for *x*.

There is a serious problem with the way algebra is often introduced in textbooks. A central idea in algebra is that of a variable, which could be *x, y,* or any other symbol. But students are not introduced to variables that can actually vary. Instead they are asked to solve for *x,* they do repeated exercises solving for *x,* and they—not surprisingly—get the idea that *x* has to be one number that does not vary. This is not a good representation of a variable. Students are usually introduced to algebra by solving for *x* in artificial situations where only one number can represent *x*. But the most critical aspect of a variable is that it is *something that varies*. When students have solved for *x* for enough hours, they become resistant to seeing algebra as something that can describe patterns and growth, with variables that vary, when this is arguably the most important part of algebra.

An example of a variable varying, which I shared in the Grade 6 book, was the growing pattern illustrated in Figure 9.1.

The shape in Figure 9.1 has a constant value of 5, shown by the green cross in the middle. But the tails of the cross grow each time, and the growth is always 2*x,*

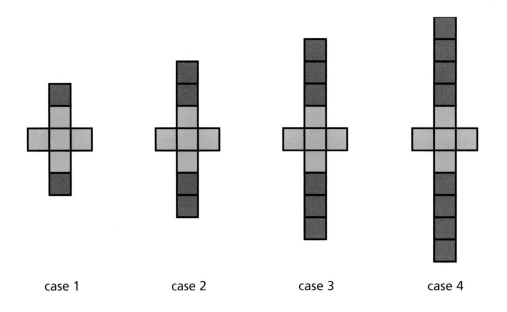

case 1   case 2   case 3   case 4

Figure 9.1   A growth pattern

two times the case number. In case 1 there are 2 squares, in case 2 there are 4, and so on. For this reason, the linear expression that describes the growth is $2x + 5$. One reason that we know this growth is linear is that a graph of the pattern growth, showing the case number against the number of squares, would be a straight line.

In the expression illustrated, the value of x changes depending on the case number. In case 1 it is 1, and in case 2 it is 2. This shows the meaning of the word *variable*—it varies. This is the very best way to introduce students to algebra—help them see that variables are useful ways to express change.

In our activities in this big idea, we show students variables that vary. We also show them algebra visually. This gives students critical insights into functional growth, which they do not get when they only encounter functions as numbers and symbols. Mathematician Steve Strogatz writes about the problems of algebra without visuals and without meaning:

> Equations could be massaged almost mindlessly, peacefully; you could add the same term to both sides of an equation, cancel common terms, solve for an unknown quantity, or perform a dozen other procedures and algorithms according to standard recipes. The process of algebra could be soothingly repetitive, like the pleasures of knitting. But algebra suffered from its emptiness. Its symbols were vacuous. They meant nothing until they were given meaning. There was nothing to visualize. Algebra was left-brained and mechanical. (2019, p. 98)

The problems Steve highlights—of algebra being empty, vacuous, meaningless, and mechanical—are completely addressed when the ideas become visual.

Our algebra activities give students opportunities to see ideas visually and to encounter variables that vary. They also invite students into a domain I rarely, if ever, see in textbooks. We ask students to think about the patterns as they move into negative space. We have found that both students and teachers are challenged and excited to think about negative growth and to consider what negative space really means.

In our Visualize activity, students will explore ways to represent growing and shrinking patterns by connecting visual representations of patterns to integers. We ask students to think of large and small cases and to use their visual thinking to work out what the cases will look like. In traditional versions of tasks like this, students are encouraged to draw up tables of numbers to try to work out patterns. We do not want this; we want students to think visually and to use that visual thinking to work out the pattern. Later they can also make tables of numbers, and connect the numbers to their visual thinking.

In our Play activity, students again see patterns visually. This time they are asked to explore similarities and differences between patterns. Pattern C is linear, and pattern D is nonlinear. Students are then invited to make their own patterns—a creative act that will generate many different and interesting patterns for the class to consider.

In our Investigate activity, students consider the growth of different letters. They explore variations in growth patterns, again seeing algebraic ideas visually, which stimulates important brain communication.

Jo Boaler

Reference

Strogatz, S. (2019). *Infinite powers: How calculus reveals the secrets of the universe.* (Advance reading copy). Boston, MA: Houghton Mifflin Harcourt.

Case by Case

Snapshot

Students explore how to represent growing and shrinking patterns by connecting visual representations of patterns to integers.

Connection to CCSS
7.EE.2, 7.EE.4, 7.NS.1, 7.RP.2a,b,c

Agenda

Activity	Time	Description/Prompt	Materials
Launch	10–15 min	Show students pattern A and ask how they see the pattern growing. Invite students to share where they see new squares being added, and color-code these different ways on the sheet. Ask students what cases 0 and –1 might look like, and give students a chance to generate some ideas.	• Pattern A Display Sheet, to display • Colors
Explore	45+ min	Using patterns A–C, partners explore what the pattern looks like when extended both left and right. Students develop ways of describing the pattern's rule of change and for predicting the number of squares in cases 100, 500, and –100.	• Pattern A, B, and C sheets, for each partnership • Colors, for each partnership • Make available: grid paper (see appendix) and square tiles
Discuss	20+ min	Discuss each pattern and how students saw it growing or shrinking. Discuss the ways that students represented the rule for the pattern's change and make connections between different representations. Compare ways that students made predictions about the number of squares in distant cases.	Pattern A, B, and C sheets, to display

BIG IDEA 9: USING ALGEBRA AS A PROBLEM-SOLVING TOOL

To the Teacher

In these patterns, we are pushing students to consider how the patterns grow or shrink across cases, and we take advantage of students' developing understanding of integers. In previous grades, we have focused on linear growth, but here in seventh grade, after the work we've done with the human number line in Big Idea 8, we want students to grapple with patterns moving in both directions, growing and shrinking. As the patterns shrink, students will need to develop ways of representing negative quantities in the patterns, which they might do with color or with the physical arrangement of the tiles. The images shown in Figure 9.2 show two ways students might represent shrink in pattern A, which the class will begin to discuss in the launch.

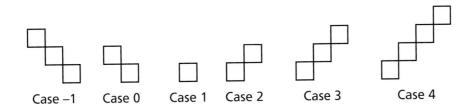

One way to continue the pattern to the 0 and negative one cases is to make a mirror image

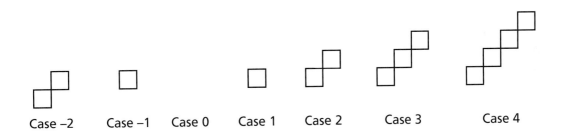

One way to continue the pattern to the 0 and negative cases is to continue the pattern growing downward to the left.

Figure 9.2

Encourage students to use color to highlight the ways they see growth or shrink in different representations of the pattern. For instance, if they use blue to show a new layer of squares, they may also want to use blue on the table or graph they construct to show this step in the growth. You can see in the introduction to this book how this helps us see patterns.

Activity

Launch

Launch the activity by showing students the Pattern A Display Sheet on the document camera and pointing out that this is a part of a pattern, from case 1 to case 4. Ask students, How do you see the pattern growing? Where do you see new squares being added? Give students a chance to turn and talk about what they notice and how they see it. Invite students to share their observations by coming up to the pattern and pointing to where they see the new squares being added in each case. Color-code the patterns to show different ways to see the growth.

Point out that the pattern can also move to the left, and we could see it as removing squares as we go from case 4 to case 3 and so on. Ask, What might case 0 look like? Or case −1? Give students a chance to turn and talk about the possibilities. Students will likely not come to agreement on what these cases look like, but this is an opportunity to discuss what they could look like and get students thinking in both directions of the pattern.

Explore

Provide partners with the Pattern A sheet and colors. Make available grid paper (see appendix) and square tiles for exploring and building the patterns. Beginning with pattern A, and moving on to patterns B and C when students are ready, groups explore the following questions:

- What does the pattern look like as it extends to the right? (cases 4, 5, and beyond)
- What does the pattern look like as it extends to the left? (cases 0, −1, and beyond)
- How could we describe the number of squares in each case?
- How could we describe the rule for the pattern's change? Explore different ways you might use words, numbers, symbols, tables, graphs, objects, or diagrams to describe the rule.
- How many squares might it take to build case 100? 500? −100? How do you know?

Students might use words, symbols, objects, diagrams, tables, or graphs to explore, build, and describe the patterns they see. Encourage students to use color to show the different ways they see the pattern growing across the cases.

Pattern B

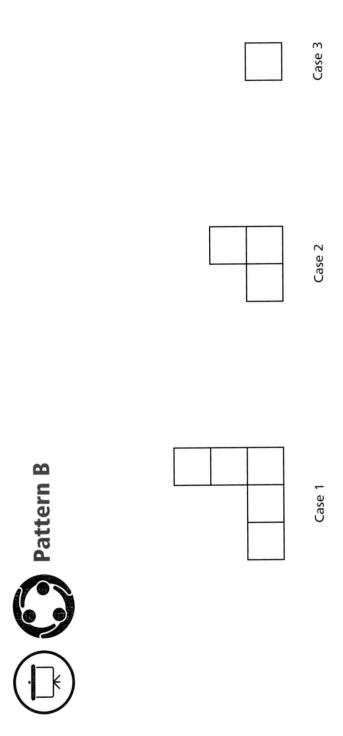

Case 1

Case 2

Case 3

Pattern C

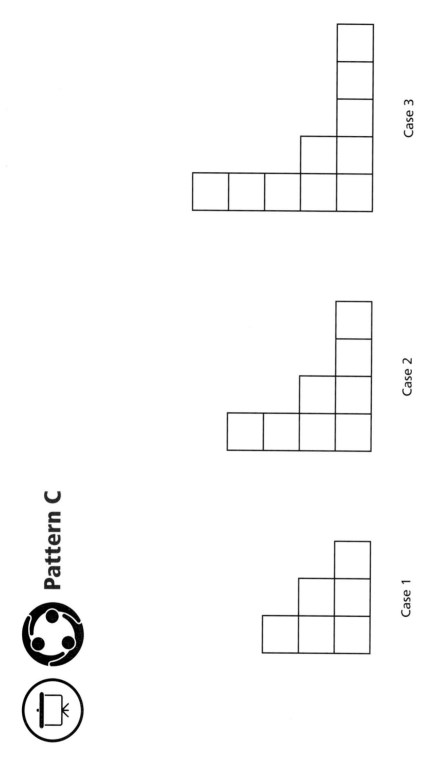

Case 1   Case 2   Case 3

(Non) Linear Pattern Puzzles

Snapshot

Students build a visual understanding of the differences between nonlinear and linear patterns and construct a pattern puzzle carnival to hunt for nonlinear patterns.

Connection to CCSS
7.RP.2a,b,c, 7.EE.2,6.RP.1

Agenda

Activity	Time	Description/Prompt	Materials
Launch	10 min	Show students the Pattern D Display Sheet and ask them how they see the pattern growing. Color-code the pattern as a class to show different ways of seeing the growth. Compare this pattern to pattern C from the Visualize activity. Ask students to think about how they are different.	• Pattern D Display Sheet, to display • Pattern C sheet from the Visualize activity, to display • Colors
Explore	20–30 min	Small groups explore the similarities and differences between pattern D and pattern C. Students find as many ways as they can to represent and describe these similarities and differences.	• Pattern D sheet, for each group • Pattern C sheet from the Visualize activity, for each group • Colors, square tiles, and grid paper (see appendix), for each group

BIG IDEA 9: USING ALGEBRA AS A PROBLEM-SOLVING TOOL

Activity	Time	Description/Prompt	Materials
Discuss	20 min	Discuss the similarities and differences between patterns D and C. Make a chart of students' findings and the ways they describe these similarities and differences. Focus attention on the differences, and name pattern D as *nonlinear* and pattern C as *linear*. Be sure that students can see the difference between these two types of patterns.	• Pattern D Display Sheet, to display • Pattern C sheet from the Visualize activity, to display • Chart and markers
Explore	30–45 min	Small groups design three visual patterns, two that are linear and one that is nonlinear. Labeling these patterns X, Y, and Z, groups post them on a chart as a puzzle for the class.	Square tiles, grid paper (see appendix), rulers, tape, chart paper, and markers, for each group
Play	30 min	Post groups' charts around the room. Host a pattern puzzle carnival in which students move from chart to chart trying to determine, Which pattern is nonlinear? How do we know? Students record their thinking about each chart as a reference for the discussion.	• Groups' charts, posted in stations around the room • Make available: square tiles, grid paper (see appendix), and colors
Discuss	15–20 min	Discuss how students identified the nonlinear patterns and any visual clues they used. Discuss, What makes a pattern nonlinear?	

To the Teacher

In the Visualize activity, we provided students with three linear patterns growing or shrinking across successive cases. Linear patterns are the focus of algebraic thinking in seventh grade; however, to identify proportional or linear relationships, students need nonlinear relationships to contrast them with. In this activity, we introduce a pattern that looks very similar to one of the patterns students explored in the previous activity, but this one is nonlinear. We invite students to use this contrast to construct and then explore the differences between linear and nonlinear patterns.

Mindset Mathematics, Grade 7

This activity will extend across at least two days, and we encourage you to give students the time they need to construct and test their patterns until they can agree that they have designed two linear and one nonlinear pattern.

Activity

Launch

Launch the activity by showing students the Pattern D Display Sheet on the document camera. Ask students, Where do you see new squares being added in each case? How do you see this pattern growing? Give students a chance to turn and talk to a partner about what they see. Invite students to come up and show how they see the growth, and color-code the changes on the pattern on the document camera.

Ask, How is this pattern different from the pattern we looked at in the Visualize activity? Show students pattern C from the Visualize activity on the document camera along with pattern D. Allows student to have a few moments to look at and think about these patterns before sending them off to work.

Explore

Provide small groups with the Pattern D sheet, the Pattern C sheet from the Visualize activity, colors, square tiles, and grid paper (see appendix). Small groups explore the following questions:

- How are the two patterns similar?
- How are the two patterns different?

Encourage students to explore the number of squares in each case and how the patterns grow. Ask students to find as many different ways to describe the similarities and differences as they can. Students can use multiple representations of the patterns to help them examine and describe similarities and differences. Students can use the work they did in the Visualize activity as a reference for pattern C.

Discuss

Show both patterns on the document camera and ask students to discuss the following questions:

- How are the two patterns similar?
- How are the two patterns different?
- What representations help you see these similarities and differences?

Make a chart to collect the ways that students describe the similarities and differences. In this discussion, focus students' attention on the ways the growth in each pattern is different and how that can be seen in the number of squares and in tables and graphs. The new pattern is not linear, and the ways students have described growth in the past (such as "add 3") do not work for this type of pattern. Name this pattern as *nonlinear* because it does not have the same growth, or rate of change, from case to case. If students have graphed the two patterns, you can also note that the graph of this pattern is a curve. Name this pattern as different from *linear* patterns, whose growth can be represented as a line, as with pattern C. Be sure that students can see the differences between these two types of patterns in students' multiple representations.

Explore

Provide groups with square tiles, grid paper (see appendix), rulers, tape, chart paper, and markers. Ask each group to design three visual patterns, each on a separate sheet of grid paper. Each pattern should show at least three cases, with each case clearly labeled. Two of these patterns must be linear, and one should be nonlinear.

Groups will likely need to experiment with patterns and discuss the growth to be sure they have created patterns that they agree are linear and nonlinear. Encourage students to build their patterns with tiles first, because these make revision simple.

When they have completed their patterns, ask students to label their patterns X, Y, and Z (in no particular order). Groups post their patterns on chart paper as a puzzle for the rest of the class. Be sure each group labels their chart with group members' names.

Play

Post groups' charts around the classroom. You might want these on the walls or at table stations. Host a pattern puzzle carnival where the goal is for groups to visit each poster and discuss the questions, Which pattern is nonlinear? How do you know?

Students rotate around the room freely with their groups, examining each chart and trying to determine which is the nonlinear pattern. Students will need access to tools for exploring these patterns, such as tiles, grid paper (see appendix), and colors. Ask groups to record their thinking about each chart so that they can remember which patterns at the stations they found to be nonlinear and why. These notes will be useful during the discussion.

Discuss

Discuss the following questions:

- How could we sort these patterns into linear and nonlinear?
- What ways did you develop to tell whether a pattern is linear or nonlinear?

If possible, pull the nonlinear patterns off each chart and relocate them together on the board. Discuss these questions:

- Are there any visual clues that a pattern is linear or nonlinear?
- What makes a pattern nonlinear?

Look-Fors

- **Do students have ways of describing the differences between a linear and nonlinear pattern?** In the initial parts of this activity, we hope that students will be able to identify some specific differences between linear and nonlinear patterns that can be generalized. Students may notice differences between the two patterns that are not inherent to linearity, such as "Pattern D has more squares than pattern C." Focus students' attention on the patterns of growth instead by asking questions that invite them to compare the changes from case to case. In this first discussion and later as you circulate while students are designing patterns, you'll want to hear how students are describing these differences and whether they make sense with the definitions of linear and nonlinear. For instance, students might informally state that "the growth gets bigger and bigger" in nonlinear patterns, or they may notice that the nonlinear pattern has a square (2 × 2, then 3 × 3, and so on) embedded in the design. While these features are not necessarily true of all nonlinear patterns, they are features that help explain why pattern D is nonlinear. At this stage, this is entirely sufficient reasoning.

- **Are students agreeing on whether a pattern is linear or nonlinear?** Listen to how groups discuss and debate the patterns they are creating for the carnival. Students may begin simply by pushing square tiles into a series of forms, without knowing immediately whether the pattern is linear or nonlinear. This is a fine approach, but it requires that groups then analyze what they have made and agree on whether it is linear or nonlinear. What reasoning are they using? Are they attending to the features of the pattern that describe its growth? Alternatively, students may design their patterns intentionally to be linear or nonlinear at the outset. If so, what criteria are they using? Ask students questions about how they created and agreed on the patterns they have made. The reasoning that students use will support the carnival and the closing discussion, where you may want to challenge students' assumptions about what qualifies as nonlinear. For instance, you could ask, Does there need to be a square embedded in the design (as there is in pattern D)?

- **Are students connecting linearity to graphing?** One key way of visualizing linear patterns and contrasting them to nonlinear patterns is to graph the number of squares in each case. Linear patterns form a line, and nonlinear patterns do not. This is not the only way of conceiving of the differences between linear and nonlinear patterns, but it is one of the clearest ways of distinguishing between them. Look for students who choose to graph the number of squares in each case to compare the two patterns, and be sure to highlight this approach during the discussions. Ask how the appearance of the graph—a line or a curve—connects back to the other representations students have used.

Reflect

How do you create a linear pattern? How do you create a nonlinear pattern?

Pattern D Display Sheet

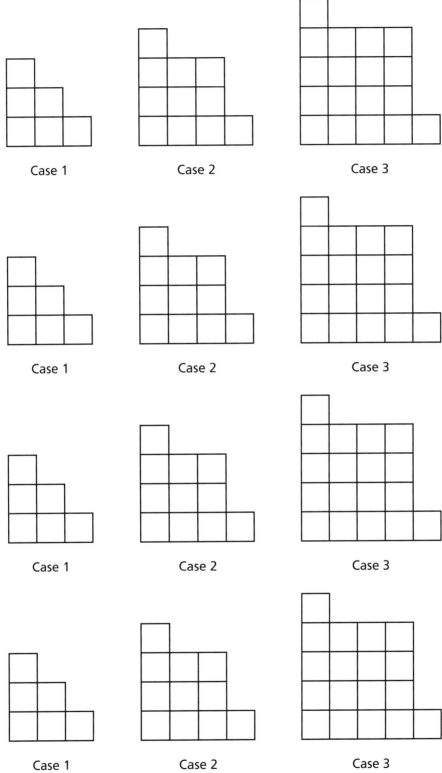

Case 1   Case 2   Case 3

Case 1   Case 2   Case 3

Case 1   Case 2   Case 3

Case 1   Case 2   Case 3

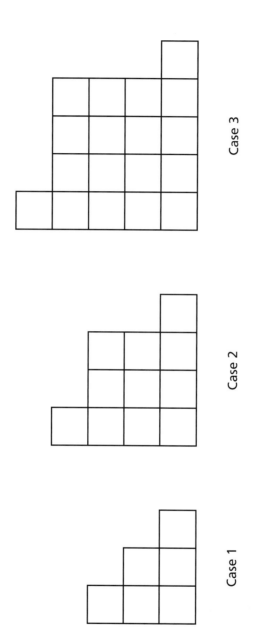

Case 3

Case 2

Case 1

Linear Letters

Snapshot

Students investigate how letters formed on a grid grow and whether these patterns of growth are always linear. Students investigate which letters grow most rapidly, or have the steepest slope.

Connection to CCSS
7.RP.2a,b,c, 7.EE.2, 7.EE.4a

Agenda

Activity	Time	Description/Prompt	Materials
Launch	10 min	Show students the Growing H sheet and ask them how they see the letter growing. Ask students how they might describe the pattern of growth using words, symbols, tables, or graphs.	Growing H sheet, to display
Explore	45+ min	Small groups investigate the H's growth to determine whether it is linear. Groups then investigate other letters and how they might grow to determine whether all letters grow linearly. For each letter that groups explore, they create a chart showing their findings. Groups investigate which letters grow most rapidly.	• Growing H sheet, for each group • Square tiles, grid paper (see appendix), charts, tape, and colors, for each group
Discuss	20+ min	Post students' charts alphabetically around the classroom. Discuss the patterns students discovered when creating growing letters. Discuss whether all letters can be made to grow linearly or not, and why. Note any differences in the ways that groups made the same letter grow and how these influence the equations, tables, or graphs for the patterns.	

To the Teacher

In this activity, we extend the work students have done so far with linear and non-linear patterns to explore the ways that letter forms on a grid might grow. We begin by looking at a simple form of the letter H and how it grows on a grid. If you look at this letter pattern the way we have with earlier growing patterns, asking, Where do I see the squares being added from case to case? you will notice that the vertices or intersection points of the H remain constant, but the length of each segment grows by one.

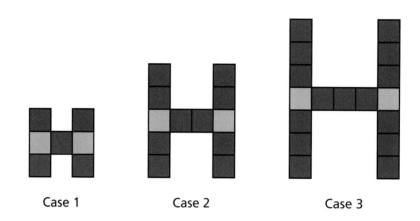

Case 1   Case 2   Case 3

The joints (green) remain constant in each case number.
The length of the segments grow.

This kind of pattern lends itself to considering the constants and the variables, along with the rate of change. Students could use this to develop an expression for the number of squares in the letter H, which could look like $2 + 5h$, where h = case number.

We invite students to investigate whether all letters, when formed on a grid, grow linearly. One thing to note is that there can be more than one way to make a letter. The letter H is fairly straightforward, because it is composed of perpendicular and parallel lines. Letters that involve curves or lines on an angle to the grid require students to solve the problem of how to fit them into the grid; students may solve these problems differently, as in the case of the letter A, shown in Figure 9.3. These are two different and valid ways of constructing growing As, provided students are consistent across the pattern. Notice, though, that the differences in the ways these are constructed will lead to different equations. In this case, changing the number of vertices reduces the number of squares that remain constant, while the rate of change remains the same.

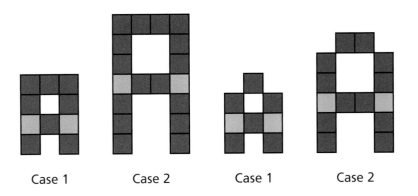

Case 1   Case 2   Case 1   Case 2

Figure 9.3   Growing A's with different visual, numerical, and algebraic representations.

Activity

Launch

Launch the activity by showing students the Growing H sheet on the document camera. Ask students, How do you see the H growing? How could we describe and show the growth using words, tables, graphs, or equations? Give students a chance to turn and talk, and then collect students' observations and their ideas for how they might explore the patterns in this letter.

Explore

Provide groups with the Growing H sheet, square tiles, grid paper (see appendix), charts, tape, and colors. Groups investigate the following questions:

- Is the H's growth linear?
- Do all letters grow linearly?
- Are there are any letters that cannot be made to grow linearly?
- How can you represent the growth of different letters using equations, tables, and graphs?
- Which letters grow most rapidly? How do you know?

Groups investigate the ways they can make a letter grow when it is made on a grid or with square tiles. Ask students to follow a few guidelines for developing growing letters. First, the letters must be formed on a grid, even when made with square tiles; this means that tiles must be square and connected along full sides or at corners. Second, students must develop a consistent pattern for growing the letter from case to case.

For each letter a group investigates, ask them to make a chart showing how it might grow from case to case and the ways the group represented its pattern of growth.

Discuss

Post students' charts alphabetically. Discuss the following questions:

- What patterns of growth did you find as you explored different letters?
- What variations in growth patterns do you notice across the alphabet?
- Did we all make the letters in the same way? Does it matter? Why or why not?
- Why do different forms of the same letter have different equations?
- Do all letters grow linearly?
- Are there are any letters that cannot be made to grow linearly?
- Which letters grow most rapidly? How do you know? (Draw attention to the way the slope of the line can help us see the rate of change and compare these across letters.)
- What representations enabled you to see linear and nonlinear growth most clearly?

If you notice, as mentioned in the To the Teacher section, that two groups made a single letter in different ways, be sure to compare these and highlight how the differences in the growth patterns lead to differences in the graph, table, and equation for each.

Look-Fors

- **Are students distinguishing between where the letter changes and what remains constant?** As with the examples shown in the To the Teacher section, parts of each letter remain constant even as the letter itself grows. The intersection points or vertices of the letter do not change; these maintain the shape of the letter. But the length of the lines that form each letter should grow in a consistent way, making it progressively wider and taller. As you observe students at work, encourage them to color-code the letters to show how they see the letter growing, which parts are changing, and which are not. Being precise about seeing the growth of the H will support students in both building and analyzing other letters. If the class as a whole is really struggling with this, you might consider holding a brief whole-class discussion just about the letter H, focusing on how students see and can describe its growth, before they move on to experimenting with other letters.

- **Are students constructing letters that grow in consistent ways?** For students to be able to analyze patterns of growth, they need to be constructing growing letters that follow a pattern. This pattern should lead to similar figures, though this is not an explicit focus of the lesson. Instead, similarity can be a useful tool for you to use to assess visually whether students are using a consistent growing pattern from case to case. If you notice that a group's letters don't appear to be changing consistently, ask questions about how they decided to make each letter and the ways it is growing. In fact, students will need to have at least an implicit pattern in mind to construct these letters, which should support students in analyzing them. Ask, What pattern did you use to grow this letter? You might say, I notice that your letters don't just look bigger; they look different. Why is that? What pattern could you use so that they look the same, just larger?

- **Are students attempting to represent their letters with equations?** Encourage students to describe the growing pattern in several ways—with words, colors, numbers, and equations. Ask students whether there is a way to represent the number of squares needed to build each letter for any case. Support students in talking about the patterns they see and moving that language into the more abstract representation of numbers and symbols. Students may use variables for the case number and the number of squares needed to build the letter, or they might use words. Either is fine because they both represent ways of generalizing across the cases of the pattern. One reason to encourage trying equations for the patterns is that they enable the class to compare patterns across the class. For instance, you might compare two different equations for the same letter, or find two identical equations for two different letters.

Reflect

Why do letters tend to grow linearly?

Growing H

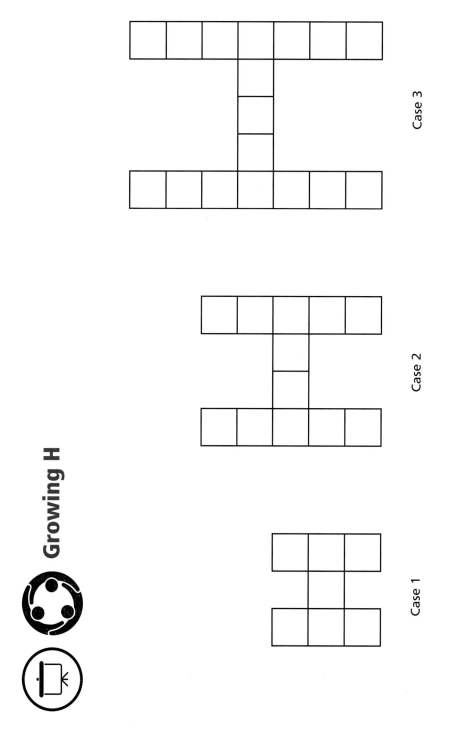

Case 1

Case 2

Case 3

BIG IDEA 10

Exploring Circles

Circles are a very special mathematical shape. One of my favorite mathematical writers, Paul Lockhart (you may have heard of his famous article, "A Mathematician's Lament"), writes that "you certainly can't ask for a prettier shape. Circles are simple, symmetrical and elegant" (2012, pp. 62–63). One of the reasons for the elegance of circles is their own unique and very special quality: all the points on a circle are the same distance from the center—a quality that no other shape shares. But there is something that is perhaps even more exciting about circles—they all contain a special relationship that we can observe in every circle in the world. If you divide the circumference of a circle by its diameter, you always get the same number, which is a little bigger than 3. This number is called pi, and it is an irrational number, which means you can never express it as two whole numbers. Many people try, by calling it $\frac{22}{7}$, but that is just an approximation. Lockhart points out that pi is not only irrational but also a number that does not satisfy any algebraic relationship at all. Such numbers are called *transcendental,* which is Latin for "climbing beyond." There are many things that are very cool about pi—it is a "transcendental" number, and, more important, it exists inside every circle in the world.

When students learn about pi they can be given the opportunity to discover its existence. I was reminded of the importance of this when I was reading a book written by science writer Margaret Wertheim. The book is not about education, but the writer recalls a powerful moment from her childhood that she describes in this way:

> When I was ten years old I had what can only be described as a mystical experience. It came during a maths class. We were learning about circles, and to his eternal credit our teacher, Mr. Marshall, let us discover for ourselves the secret of this unique shape: the number known as pi. Almost everything you want to say about circles can be said in terms of pi, and it seemed to me in my childhood innocence

that a great treasure of the universe had been revealed. Everywhere I looked I saw circles, and at the heart of every one of them was this mysterious number . . . It was as if someone had lifted a veil and shown me a glimpse of a marvelous realm beyond the one I experienced with my senses. (Wertheim, 1997, p. 3)

I have taught pi to many students, and I always design activities that enable students to discover this important relationship. Many students in the US think of pi as a really long number, often because they have been encouraged to memorize as many digits as possible. But the most important aspect of pi, in my view, is the relationship it reveals about circles. In our Visualize activity, students should be given a range of different circles and asked to measure the circumference and the diameter. The goal is for them to notice that the circumference is roughly three times the diameter, in every case. We intend for this to lead into a discussion of our transcendental number—pi.

In our Play activity, students will be challenged to think about the area of circles and to return to their special number—pi—that helps us find areas. Instead of simply telling students the area formula, we encourage them to explore the meaning of the formula and understand why it works. They will do this by considering the square of the radius, look at what that square looks like, and consider its role in the formula πr^2.

In the Investigate activity, we extend to the circular relationships found inside rolls of materials—foam rolls or paper towel rolls, for example. What do we know about circles that could help us find the length of a roll? Encourage students to use one of the most helpful mathematical approaches they can learn—estimation. How do they deal with the spiral nature of the material being wrapped around the center? This complicates their estimates in interesting ways, and makes the question different from one that involves multiple circles being stacked on top of each other. There is much to consider, explore, and investigate, making use of the circular relationships students are learning.

Jo Boaler

References

Lockhart, P. (2012). *Measurement*. Boston MA: Harvard University Press.

Wertheim, M. (1997). *Pythagoras' trousers: God, physics, and the gender wars*. New York, NY: Crown Publishing.

Building Hunches about Circumference

Snapshot

Students build hunches about the relationship between the diameter and circumference of a circle by measuring several objects with adding machine tape and looking for patterns.

Connection to CCSS
7.G.4

Agenda

Activity	Time	Description/Prompt	Materials
Launch	10 min	Show students the collection of circular objects you've gathered. Remind them of the work they did in previous years with the perimeter of polygons, and ask, How might we find the perimeter of a circular object? Collect some ideas and introduce adding machine tape as a tool.	Collection of 12–20+ everyday circular objects
Explore	15 min	Partners measure the diameter and circumference of several circles and record the results for each on a strip of adding machine tape.	• Roll or long section of adding machine tape, scissors, and markers, for each partnership • Make available: collection of 12–20+ everyday circular objects
Discuss	15 min	Post students' adding machine tape measures one above the other with the ends aligned. Discuss the patterns students notice. Make and record conjectures about the relationship between diameter and circumference.	• Space to post students' adding machine tape measures • Optional: chart and markers

Activity	Time	Description/Prompt	Materials
Explore	20 min	Partners test the class's conjectures by remeasuring the objects with greater precision. Using rulers, students record the lengths of the diameter and circumference on new pieces of adding machine tape. Partners use this evidence to support or refine the class's conjectures.	• Roll or long section of adding machine tape, scissors, rulers, and markers, for each group • Make available: collection of 12–20+ everyday circular objects
Discuss	15 min	Partners post their more precise adding machine tape measures and add their data to a class chart of objects, diameters, and circumferences. Discuss this new evidence to support or refine the class conjectures about the relationship between diameter and circumference. Discuss pi, if a desire for precision emerges from the discussion.	• Space to post students' adding machine tape measures • Chart and markers

To the Teacher

For this activity, you will need to gather some circular objects for students to explore. These should be circles or cylinders, but not spheres, which are too challenging to measure with any accuracy for our purposes. We suggest ordinary solid items such as canned goods, plates, mugs, cups, wastepaper baskets, canisters, or Frisbees. Be sure your collection varies in size and includes at least a dozen different circles.

Standards for circumference and area of circles often focus on knowing formulas, which we think is far too shallow. We want students to develop intuition about circles that matches and connects with their deep understanding of the perimeter and area of polygons. To support this goal, this lesson is about developing hunches and exploring patterns. Students have a lot of experience exploring, detecting, and describing patterns, which we hope to leverage in this lesson. It is enough if students at this stage simply notice that circumference (or the perimeter of a circle) is about triple the diameter. As we move into the Play and Investigate activities, students can come back to and define these relationships with greater precision and name pi. Some students may be familiar with pi, at least in name, and you'll need to be prepared to refocus students on what this constant actually means.

To build hunches about circumference, we return to using adding machine tape as a way of surrounding circular objects and recording their measurements. For each object students measure, they should record both the diameter and the circumference on the same piece of adding machine tape, as shown in Figure 10.1. Students can simply cut the adding machine tape so that it is the precise distance around the circle, and students should label these with the object's name.

Figure 10.1   **The adding machine tape is the length of the circumference. Each fold line shows the length of the diameter.**

Activity

Launch

Launch the activity by showing students the variety of circular objects that you have gathered, such as plates, wastepaper baskets, mugs, or cans. Remind students that they have been working on ideas about perimeter, or the distance around shapes, for years. But these explorations have always focused on polygons—shapes with straight sides where we can hold up a ruler to the sides or count their lengths.

Ask, How do we find the perimeter of a circle? Give students a chance to turn and talk to a partner. Then collect some ideas from students. Be sure to draw attention to ideas for measuring that surround the object, such as using string.

Tell students that today they will be trying this with adding machine tape and looking for patterns in the perimeter of a circle, or what we call the *circumference,* and the only straight measure of a circle that we typically use, the *diameter,* or the distance across.

Explore

Provide partners with a roll or long section of adding machine tape, markers, scissors, and access to circular objects. Groups use adding machine tape to measure the distance around a circle, and then mark and cut the paper to match the circumference. Groups mark on the same paper strip the distance across the circle, the diameter. Label each paper with the name of the object measured. Groups should be able to generate measurements for several circles.

Note that some circular objects you have available may actually be sections of cones, with a circular base and circular top that have different circumferences and diameters (such as a wastepaper basket). Students can measure these twice and create two different strips, one for the top and one for the bottom.

Discuss

Post groups' adding machine tape measures on the wall so that the starting points all align. You may want to arrange these in order of length, though it is not necessary.

Invite the class to look at this display of circumferences and diameters and discuss the following questions:

- What patterns do you notice?
- What do you think the relationship between the diameter and the perimeter (circumference) might be?

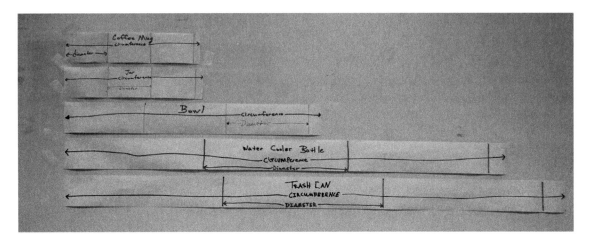

The length of the tapes show the circumference of the item measured. The fold lines show three lengths of the diameter. In each case there is a little bit left over.

In this discussion, develop one or more conjectures about the relationship between diameter and circumference to test as a class. Record these on a chart or on the board as a shared reference. At this point students might observe that the diameter is about one third of the circumference or, conversely, that the circumference is about three times the length of the diameter.

Explore

Send students back to test, by measuring more precisely, the conjectures they developed. Provide students with rulers, additional adding machine tape, scissors, and markers. Ask students to remeasure the circumference and diameters of several objects and make new strips for each. Students should label the measures for each to determine, with greater precision, whether the class's conjectures are true, or how they might revise those ideas.

Discuss

Invite students to post their more precise strips. As partners put these up on the wall, create a class table showing the name of the object and its diameter and circumference. With this more precise data, discuss the following questions:

- What evidence do we have to support or refute our conjectures?
- What do we now think might be the relationship between diameter and circumference?
- What evidence can we use to support this pattern?

If students are moving toward precision in describing this relationship—for instance, by using calculators to investigate the ratio—then use this moment to build on their interest to define this number as *pi*. Pi is the relationship between diameter and circumference, and no matter the size of the circle, the circumference is always a little more than three times (or pi times) the length of the diameter. However, if students converge instead on the idea that circumference is about three times the diameter, then encourage them to focus instead on how consistent this relationship is no matter the size of the circle.

Look-Fors

- **Do students understand why finding the perimeter of a circle is different from doing so with polygons?** At the root of the challenges with circles, which are treated as different from all other shapes, is the curve. Much attention is given to polygons in earlier grades, and students are asked to ignore the complexities of curves. Then, in seventh grade, circles are suddenly introduced in isolation. Even the language of circles is different—circumference versus perimeter and diameter versus length, width, or height. This conceptual and linguistic isolation can lead students to thinking of circles as unrelated to polygons, when, in fact, the notions of perimeter and area are entirely the same. Students need to see this connection and understand why the curves of a circle necessitate different approaches to finding the same measures they have been finding for years with polygons. Consider asking students directly in the launch why they think we need to develop strategies for and ideas about the perimeter of a circle that are different from polygons. Do students see that the curves make measurement harder? You may need to push the motivation for developing methods for finding circumference by asking, How can we ever be precise about the circumference when measuring a curve is so hard?

- **Does pi come up in conversation? How are students understanding pi?** Be listening for students who start offering pi, or even formulas for the circumference (or area) of a circle, as solutions during this activity. Many of your students may have heard of pi, or the formulas, but few, if any, will understand what pi represents. This activity is designed to support students in being able to visualize pi as a relationship between diameter and circumference, rather than to parrot a string of symbols. If students offer pi, you might ask direct questions that probe how they understand pi. Students will likely not be able to fully explain this idea, and you can point out that if they don't understand what pi is, then they should explore the relationships they can see and explain. Promise to return to this idea when it has meaning for everyone, and then be sure to tackle it at the very end of the final discussion.

- **How precise are students being when recording measures of objects with a ruler?** Encourage students to be as precise as possible when measuring their adding machine tape during the second part of the activity. For students to detect the difference between circumference being "three times" and "a little more than three times" the diameter, measurements will need to be careful. You might encourage students to use centimeters as a unit, because the smaller unit size and the metric system enable students to measure with greater precision. When you facilitate the closing discussion and students are testing the relationship between diameter and circumference, students may notice variation in the relationship if they use calculators to divide the two measures. Be sure to ask questions about the source of this variation, such as, Why do you think the relationship is not the same for all of our measures? Does this disprove our conjectures? Why or why not?

Reflect

How can you find the circumference of a circle?

Dissecting Circle Area

Snapshot

Students explore the formula for the area of a circle and build visual representations of what it means.

Connection to CCSS
7.G.4

Agenda

Activity	Time	Description/Prompt	Materials
Launch	10 min	Remind students of the relationship they found between circumference and diameter in the Visualize activity: pi. Tell them pi is part of the area of a circle, which can be written as: Area of a circle = pi × radius² or $A = \pi r^2$. Ask, What do you think this means? Discuss students' ideas and interpretations.	
Play	30+ min	Partners use the circles on the Sample Circles sheet or ones they draw themselves to explore what the formula for area of a circle means. Students try to find the areas of these circles and visually represent why the relationship in the formula between pi, the radius squared, and the area is true.	• Sample Circles sheet, grid paper (see appendix), and colors, for each partnership • Make available: scissors, glue, and compasses
Discuss	20 min	Partners share their visual representations of the formula for the area of a circle. Discuss how students made sense of and represented the different parts of the formula, and how pi is connected to area.	

Activity	Time	Description/Prompt	Materials
Extend	30–45 min	Partners use circle resources to compare the formulas for area and circumference of a circle and develop reasoning about the differences between them. Students compare these patterns to finding area and perimeter of polygons.	Sample Circles sheet, circular objects in the classroom, or tools for constructing circles, for each partnership

To the Teacher

What is a radius squared? Why would pi times the radius squared give you the area of a circle? Have you ever asked these questions? Perhaps not. The meaning of the area of a circle is not intuitive, and we don't expect students to invent or discover this relationship as they did with circumference. Rather, we want students to make sense of the formula for area and develop visual representations of what it means. Students will likely understand what the area of a circle is conceptually—the number of square units needed to cover the circle. And we hope that after the Visualize lesson, they will have a beginning understanding of pi. But the radius squared is a mystery, and we encourage you to focus students' attention on trying to represent this idea visually as a key to understanding the formula for area.

The radius squared can be seen as a square with side lengths equal to the radius. It can be represented on a circle as a box with one vertex at the circle's center, two vertices on the circle's edge, and the last vertex floating outside the circle entirely, as shown in Figure 10.2.

The formula for the area of a circle says that the area of the circle is a little more than three (or pi) times the size of these squares. This is one way of thinking about what the formula is saying. But how can this be true? The radius square extends beyond the circle itself. Students might tackle testing this idea by focusing on how to fit three radius squares into a circle. Students might notice the portion of the radius square that is outside the circle and try to find out how big it is, to subtract it away from the four radius squares that cover a circle completely. In this activity, we are inviting students into the formula in a way that is rarely done, and asking them to tackle its meaning by drawing, counting, decomposing, and transforming circles.

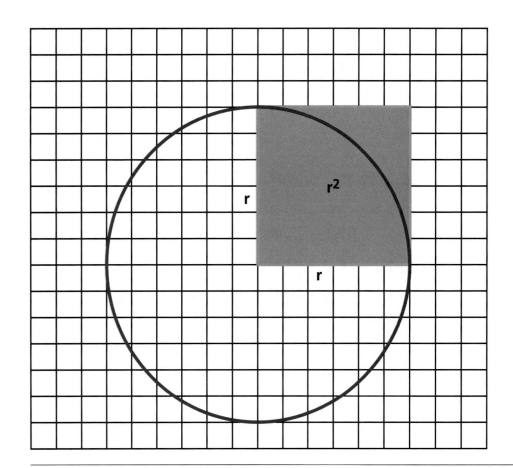

Figure 10.2 A visual showing a square with side lengths equal to the radius of the circle.

Activity

Launch

Launch the activity by reminding students of the work they did in the Visualize activity and that they found a relationship between the diameter of a circle and its circumference. That relationship is *pi*. That is to say, the circumference is a little more than three times the length of the diameter, every time, no matter the size of the circle.

Tell students that it turns out there is a pi relationship in the area of a circle as well. We've found that no matter the size of the circle, its area is pi times the radius squared. Show students that this can be written as follows:

$$\text{Area of a circle} = \text{pi} \times \text{radius}^2 \text{ or } A = \pi r^2$$

Ask students, What do you think this means? Give students a chance to turn and talk to a partner, and then invite them to share some interpretations. Be open to all the ways students might stumble through making sense of this very abstract idea.

Explore

Provide partners with copies of the Sample Circles sheet, grid paper (see appendix), and colors, and access to scissors, glue, and compass. Partners work to explore the following questions:

- How can you find the area of a circle?
- What does it mean that the area of a circle is pi times the radius squared?
- How can you construct a visual representation of this relationship?
- What evidence can you find that this relationship is true?

Students can use the circles provided or construct their own circles to explore and test their ideas. Partners develop a visual representation of what the formula for the area of a circle means that they can share with the class.

Note that if groups seem stuck as they are developing their ways of visualizing the area relationship, you may want to pause the class to invite students to share how they are getting started or the initial ideas they have had about representing circle area. This may help share and spread ideas.

Discuss

Invite each group to present their visual representations of the area of the circle. Ask each group to explain how they thought about drawing or showing why the area of a circle can be thought of as pi times the radius squared. Discuss the following questions as students share their representations:

- How did you make sense of the parts of the area equation (pi and r^2)?
- What is the radius squared? What does it look like?
- How is pi connected to area?

Be sure to highlight representations and ideas that specifically show the square that the radius can make and how it can be used to find the area of the circle.

Extend

Invite students to explore the two pi patterns in circles: $C = \pi D = 2\pi r$ and $A = \pi r^2$. Provide partners with the Sample Circles sheet, circular objects in the classroom, or tools for constructing circles. Ask students to explore the following questions:

- Why are these relationships different?
- Why does one involve squaring the radius and the other does not?
- How are these patterns for finding the perimeter and area of circles similar to those we use for finding the perimeter and area of polygons?
- How are they different? Why are they different?

After students have had a chance to explore these two formulas side by side, discuss students' findings and the comparisons they can draw between these two formulas.

Look-Fors

- **Are students interpreting the radius squared as a square?** When we use the language of "squared," it suggests an action, which student learn to associate with multiplication. But the term literally means to construct a square with the side length being "squared" and to find the area of this shape. We want students to connect these two ideas of "squared"—multiplying a quantity by itself, and the area of a square—to help them represent this part of the formula visually. Ask students direct questions about the meaning of this part of the formula, such as, What does "radius squared" mean? What might a "radius squared" look like? Where could you find a "radius squared" in these pictures of circles?

- **Are student thinking about pi times the radius squared as approximately three squares?** Pi is another abstract concept in this formula. Although students have laid a foundation for pi as the relationship between diameter and circumference, with a value a little larger than 3, this may seem distant from finding area. Ask students how they are interpreting this part of the formula, once they have made strides in visualizing the radius squared. Ask, What does it mean that we multiply the radius squared by pi? How could we describe this in other words? How could you show pi times the radius squared on a square? Support students in thinking of pi as a number, and that this number describes how many radius squares are needed to cover a circle completely.

- **How are students counting and comparing area across different circles?** The activity does not ask students to find the areas of circles directly. Rather students are focusing on making meaning of the formula. However, to make meaning, students will likely benefit from testing out ideas on a specific circle or two and actually counting the area using the grid provided. Notice how students tackle this work. How are they dealing with the curve? Are students counting the radius squared? How are they decomposing the part of the radius square that is inside the circle from the part that is outside? Ask students questions about how they are deciding what to count and what it means for area and for the formula.

- **If students are constructing their own circles, are they making ones that are useful for investigation?** We've created space for students to construct and test any circles they want in this activity. However, some circles are easier to explore than others. The circles we've provided on the Sample Circles sheet all have a center positioned at an intersection on the grid, with a radius that is a whole number of units. This makes finding and counting the radius square more straightforward. We don't want students to get bogged down trying to find the center and radius. If students make their own circles, they may not be strategic in drawing them and may inadvertently make exploring their own circles quite challenging. If you notice that groups have made challenging circles, you might encourage them to start with the Sample Circles and then test their ideas on circles they create. Once students build some ideas about how to interpret the formula, they are more likely to want to test those ideas intentionally.

Reflect

What is pi?

 **Sample Circles**

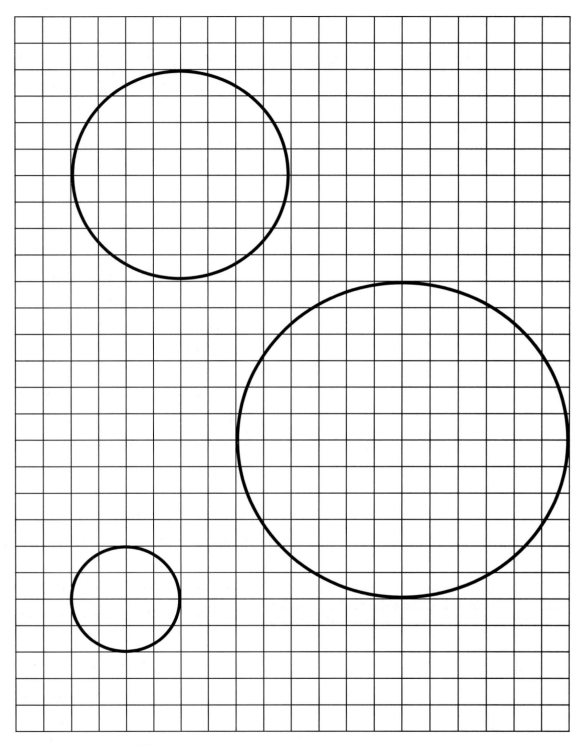

Unraveling Circles

Snapshot

Students investigate the length of a roll of foam, exploring the connection between the circumference and area of a circle.

Connection to CCSS
7.G.4

Agenda

Activity	Time	Description/Prompt	Materials
Launch	10 min	Show students the Field Hockey Foam Roll image and tell them that it is a roll of foam to pad a new field hockey field. Ask students, About how long is this roll of foam? What would you need to do to figure it out? Give students a chance to develop some ideas and collect their thoughts about getting started.	Field Hockey Foam Roll sheet, to display
Explore	45+ min	Small groups investigate the length of the field hockey foam roll, and use modeling to develop methods for estimating its length.	• Field Hockey Foam Roll sheet, for each group • Make available: materials for modeling (see To the Teacher section)
Discuss	20 min	Discuss the methods students developed for estimating the length of the foam roll. Debate which methods, or combination of methods, might lead to the most accurate estimate. Make connections between circumference, area, diameter, and radius.	

To the Teacher

In this activity, we invite students to move beyond the formulas for the area and circumference of circles and tackle a task that involves estimating with both. When the Stanford Women's Field Hockey field needed to be resurfaced, we saw these enormous rolls of foam stacked nearby, ready to be unrolled across the vast space. It was staggering how many of these giant rolls were needed for this task. This got us wondering about the connection between the area (of the end of the cylinder) and circumference (as the foam spirals around the edge of the ever-growing circle). In this investigation, we ask students to estimate the length of the foam on one of these rolls, a task that students might approach using either circumference or area as a starting point.

We emphasize that what students are developing is an estimate, as they have no ready mathematical tools for calculating precisely. Estimation opens up a much-needed space for genuine mathematical debate. No one can be precisely right; students instead can argue for why one method might lead to a more accurate solution. In fact, your class might find that combining methods would lead to the most accurate approach. Discussions of estimations enable you to focus on the methods and the conceptual reasoning that supports them.

To develop ideas about how to solve this problem, students may want to simulate the roll of foam using something physical, and you'll need appropriate materials on hand. To simulate the foam roll in the picture, you'll want something that has a hollow core and a material thick enough that students can count the layers as they are added. Rolls of paper towels or thicker toilet paper can be useful. Alternatively, you might offer a tube and thin foam that students can roll around it as they explore what happens.

Activity

Launch

Launch the activity by showing the Field Hockey Foam Roll image on the document camera. Tell students that this roll of foam was being used to pad a field hockey field. The foam is 1″ thick, and it is rolled around a tube that is 4″ in diameter. Ask the questions, About how long is this roll of foam? How could you figure it out? What would you need to know or do? Give students a chance to turn and talk to a partner about their ideas. Students may need a longer time to talk to come up with some ideas. Ask students to share some things they would need to figure out to determine the length of the roll.

Explore

Provide groups with a copy of the Field Hockey Foam Roll image. Provide access to materials for modeling this problem, such as rolls of paper towels or toilet paper, or extra tubes and foam they can roll themselves. Groups investigate the following questions:

- What is happening as the foam is rolled around the tube?
- How can you use what you know about circumference to help you think about the length of the foam on this roll?
- What do you need to figure out to find its length?
- How can you model this situation with other materials to help you think about the length of the foam?
- About how long is this roll of foam? How do you know?

After students develop some ideas about the length of the roll, you might ask students to investigate the question, If the rolls are each 10 feet wide, how large an area will one roll cover?

Discuss

Discuss the following questions:

- What methods did you develop to find the length of the foam roll?
- How did you model this situation? How did your models help you?
- How precise do you think your estimate is?
- (Invite groups to share their different estimates and methods for finding them.) What do we learn by looking across the estimates in the class? What do we now think is the most likely length of the roll, based on everyone's work?
- What made finding the length challenging?
- How did you use circumference? What was happening to the radius, diameter, and circumference in this roll? How did you use this to help you think about length?

If students have investigated the area of the roll, invite them to share their findings and discuss the following questions:

- What methods did you develop for finding the area?
- How were your methods for finding area different from or similar to your methods for finding the length of the roll? Why?
- How were your methods for finding area different from or similar to your methods for finding the area of a circle? Why?

Look-Fors

- **How are students dealing with precision?** Precision plays an interesting role in estimation tasks. On the one hand, students are expected to estimate the length of the roll and not find a precise answer. Students should recognize that the formula for circumference will not accurately reflect the length of a section of a spiral. On the other hand, students should make efforts in their methods to be precise about those measurements that allow for precision. For instance, students can count the layers in the photograph of the foam roll with accuracy, and the thickness of that foam is provided. As students estimate, ask questions about the quantities and relationships students are using, such as, How do you know the length/quantity/measure? Did you count/measure or estimate? Expect that students should use precision when it is possible, and estimate when it is not.

- **How are students addressing the spiral of the roll? Are they noticing that the diameter (and therefore the circumference) is changing?** The key difference between this task and a typical circumference task is that the roll is a spiral, not a circle or set of concentric circles. As you observe students, look for evidence that students recognize the roll as a spiral and are developing methods that might use what they know about circles to tackle the task. You might ask, Is this a circle? Why does it matter that it is a spiral? As the foam gets wrapped around the roll, what changes? How can you deal with that in your method?

- **How are students modeling the task? How are students connecting their models back to the task?** For many students, modeling this task may be the key to developing methods. The physical models we have suggested, such as rolls of paper towels or foam and a cardboard tube, offer the opportunity for students to roll, unroll, and measure the material. As you observe groups, look for the ways students are using these materials and how they might be using them to test ideas. For instance, students might unroll five or six rounds of paper toweling and measure the resulting length of paper and then compare that to the circumference at the outer edge of the roll multiplied by the number of rounds. Students can compare these measurements to see whether they are the same or to quantify the difference. Students might remove all the paper toweling to add back the same number of layers as in the picture of the foam roll to watch what happens to the circumference, and use that to develop a strategy. Ask students questions about what they are doing and why it will help them think about the foam roll. These models should support students in thinking about how to approximate the length of the roll in the picture, rather than getting them bogged down rolling and unrolling paper towels.

Reflect

What questions do you have about circles?

Field Hockey Foam Roll

Mindset Mathematics, Grade 7, copyright © 2019 by Jo Boaler, Jen Munson, Cathy Williams. Reproduced by permission of John Wiley & Sons, Inc.

Appendix

Centimeter Grid Paper

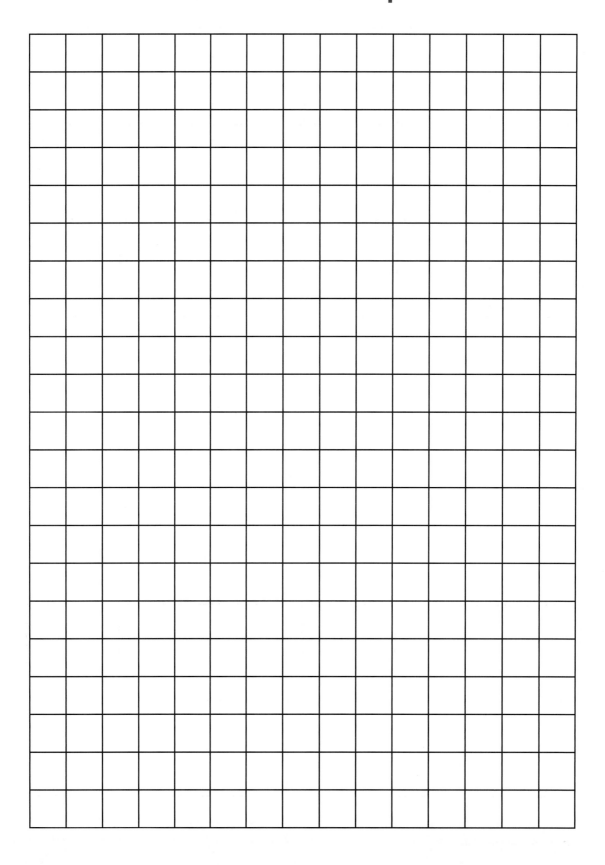

Appendix

1" Grid Paper

Snap Cube Grid Paper

Appendix

Isometric Dot Paper

Dot Paper

About the Authors

Dr. Jo Boaler is a professor of mathematics education at Stanford University, and the cofounder of Youcubed. She is the author of the first MOOC on mathematics teaching and learning. Former roles have included being the Marie Curie Professor of Mathematics Education in England, a mathematics teacher in London comprehensive schools, and a lecturer and researcher at King's College, London. Her work has been published in the *Times,* the *Telegraph,* the *Wall Street Journal,* and many other news outlets. The BBC recently named Jo one of the eight educators "changing the face of education."

Jen Munson is an assistant professor of learning sciences at Northwestern University, a professional developer, and a former classroom teacher. She received her PhD from Stanford University. Her research focuses on how coaching can support teachers in growing their mathematics instructional practices and how teacher-student interactions influence equitable math learning. She is the author of *In the Moment: Conferring in the Elementary Math Classroom*, published by Heinemann.

Cathy Williams is the cofounder and director of Youcubed. She completed an applied mathematics major at University of California, San Diego before becoming a high school math teacher for 18 years in San Diego County. After teaching, she became a county office coordinator and then district mathematics director. As part of her leadership work, Cathy has designed professional development and curriculum. Her district work in the Vista Unified School District won a California Golden Bell for instruction in 2013 for the K–12 Innovation Cohort in mathematics. In Vista, Cathy worked with Jo changing the way mathematics was taught across the district.

Acknowledgments

We thank Jill Marsal, our book agent, and the team at Wiley for their efforts to make these books what we'd imagined. We are also very grateful to our Youcubed army of teachers. Thanks to Robin Anderson for drawing the network diagram on our cover. Finally, we thank our children—and dogs!—for putting up with our absences from family life as we worked to bring our vision of mathematical mindset tasks to life.

Index

Diagrams, 57, 111, 166–167

Diameters, 253, 257. *See also* Circles

Dice, 18, 131–135, 155, 160

Discussions: of accuracy, 186; from Building Intuition about Probability, 123–124, 133–134, 139–141; about conjectures, 230; from Connecting 2D and 3D Worlds, 32, 36–37, 37, 43–44; from Constructing Figures to Scale, 52, 57, 65–66; about estimates, 187–188; from Exploring Circles, 256–258, 263, 269–270; in group work, 217; hypotheses for, 34, 36; from Modeling Probabilities, 150, 158, 167–168; about observations, 87; from Operating with Opposites, 203–205, 210, 219–220; from Sampling to Understand Populations, 176, 182–184, 188–189; from Seeing Proportional Relationships, 75, 82, 88–89; of strategies, 173, 208; from Understanding Percents in the World, 97–98, 105–106, 113–114; from Using Algebra as a Problem-Solving Tool, 231, 239–241, 248

Dissecting Circle Area (lesson), 260–266

Division, 218–220, 224. *See also* Multiplication

Documentation, 190

Dot paper, 31–32, 42–43, 167, 277–278

Drawing, 52–53, 65, 158

Driscoll, Mark, 8

Duckworth, Eleanor, 48

E

Ecosystems, 51

Education, 9, 11–12, 251–252

Einstein, Albert, 13–14

Encountering Percents, 109, 112, 117–118

Endangered animals, 51

Engagement, 2–3

Environment, 21

Equations, 226–227, 246, 249

Equivalent ratios, 111

Estimates, 119, 176–177, 181, 184, 186–190, 268

Experimentation: chance and, 141–142; designs as, 210; in math, 145–146; by students, 140–141, 150–151; theory and, 147, 151

Explanations, 152

Exploration: in Building Intuition about Probability, 123, 139; of chance, 131; in Connecting 2D and 3D Worlds, 31–32, 36, 42–43; in Constructing Figures to Scale, 52, 64–65; of data, 138; of formulas, 260; as group work, 36–37, 72, 147, 166–167, 237, 256–257, 263, 269; learning from, 268; in Modeling Probabilities, 149–150, 167; of money, 104–105; in Operating with Opposites, 203–205, 219; of patterns, 228; predictions and, 136; in Sampling to Understand Populations, 175–176, 188; in Seeing Proportional Relationships, 74, 88; Slice Hypotheses Sheet for, 36, 39; in Understanding Percents in the World, 97, 112; in Using Algebra as a Problem-Solving Tool, 230, 239–240, 247–248

Exploring Circles: agendas for, 253–254, 260–261, 267; discussions from, 256–258, 263, 269–270;

World for, 103; play in, 136–137; predictions in, 123, 157–158; presentations of, 98; for proportions, 175–176; questions for, 57, 64–65, 97, 132, 140, 166, 219–220; situations for, 109, 112; for students, 42–44, 52, 199; testing and, 35; visualization in, 239

Growing A's (game), 246–247

Growing Dough (lesson), 72–79

Growing H, 250

Growth patterns, 226

Guessing, 210–211

H

Harvey Mudd College, 197

"The Having of Wonderful Ideas" (Duckworth), 48

High-ceiling tasks, 2–3

How Close to 100, 2–3

Huichol beadwork rhino, 173–177, 179

Human number lines, 199–206

Humphreys, Cathy, 8, 104

Hunches, 253–255

Hypotheses, 34, 36, 39

I

Images: conclusions from, 187–188; estimates about, 190; extensions with, 96–97; A Fishy Image, 55–60; for group work, 188; learning with, 58; relational approach for, 52–53

Imagination, 81, 175

Impossibility, 140–141

Inferences, 52, 180

Integer Tic-Tac-Toe (lesson), 207–215

Integers: integer operations, 216–221; Integer Tic-Tac-Toe, 207–215; learning, 199–206

Interpretations, 32, 264

Intuition: chance and, 124, 142; investigation and, 138; polygons and, 261; for probability, 119–120; for scaling measurements, 56; of students, 51, 121. *See also* Building Intuition about Probability

Investigation, 9; of area, 267; of compound probabilities, 168; conjectures after, 120; of designs, 173; in group work, 88, 245, 247–248, 267; intuition and, 138; launches for, 28; for learning, 14–15; manipulatives for, 146; in math, 164–166; of methodology, 94, 186; for multiplication, 198; patterns in, 110, 172; of play, 189; questions for, 187–188; of relationships, 252; by students, 89, 163, 245; of units, 265

Is It Fair? (lesson), 121–130

Is It Proportional? (lesson), 80–85

Isometric Dot Paper, 167, 277

Isometric geoboards. *See* Galton Boards

J

Jenkins, Steve, 81

Journals, 5–6

K

Kinetic learning, 27–28, 30, 197–206

Kinetic sand, 19, 35

L

Labeling, 76, 83, 106, 240, 256

Language: of math, 97–98, 247, 258–259; numbers as, 140–141; of pi, 258; of populations, 174; of probability, 135; of theory, 152

Launches: Building Intuition about Probability, 123, 132, 138; Connecting 2D and 3D Worlds, 31, 36, 42;

Paper towel rolls, 19, 267–271

Parents, 12

Parker, Ruth, 104

Partners. *See* Group work

Pascal's triangle, 165

Patterns: for area, 48; change in, 247–248; constant values in, 249; exploration of, 228; on grid paper, 134; growth patterns, 226; in investigation, 110, 172; learning and, 33, 37, 64, 67, 75, 210, 219, 232; observations from, 65, 201–202, 211, 253; Pattern A, 234; Pattern A Display Sheet, 233; Pattern B, 235; Pattern C, 236; Pattern D, 244; Pattern D Display Sheet, 243; with pi, 264; from Playing with Data Sets, 82; questions about, 241; relationships in, 256–257; rules and, 231; in surface area, 66; symbols and, 246; visualization of, 220–221, 237, 237–239. *See also* Using algebra as a problem-solving tool

Pentagons, 41

Percentages, 93–94;

Building Benchmarks, 103–108; Painting Percents, 95–102; Two Uses of Percents, 109, 112, 116; What's it Going to Cost?, 109–118

Percents in the World, 103, 103–105, 108

Perimeters, 254–255

Pi, 251–252, 258–259, 261–263, 264. *See also* Circles

Pipe cleaners, 166

PISA. *See* Program for International Student Assessment

Pizza Dough Graph, 72, 79

Pizza Dough Recipe, 72, 77

Pizza Dough Table, 72, 78

Planning, by students, 183, 189–190

Play, 9; for Building Intuition about Probability, 132, 134; challenges in, 187; with clay objects, 28; conclusions from, 190; for Connecting 2D and 3D Worlds, 36–37; for Constructing Figures to Scale, 57; with Galton Boards, 146, 163–170; in group work, 136–137; investigation of, 189; for learning, 13–14, 198; in Modeling Probabilities,

157–158; for Operating with Opposites, 209; Playing with Clay, 34–39; Playing with Data Sets, 80, 82, 85; in Sampling to Understand Populations, 182–183; for students, 81, 94, 105, 120, 146, 172, 208, 252; in Using Algebra as a Problem-Solving Tool, 240; visualization and, 49

Playing with Clay (lesson), 34–39

Polygons, 258, 261

Populations, 171–179; Catch and Release, 180–185; Wildlife Populations, 186–195

Positive numbers. *See* Integers

Possibility, 134, 159. *See also* Probability

Posters, 21, 43–44

Precision: with data, 257–259; in learning, 66, 114, 169, 254; by students, 53, 167–168, 177, 248–249, 270

Predictions: conceptualization in, 156; of data, 83, 125; of designs, 175; exploration and, 136; in group work, 123, 157–158; in learning, 31, 165–166;

150, 251; visualization of, 262–263. *See also* Seeing proportional relationships

Representations, 249

Research, 1, 9–14, 17, 27–28

Rulers, 18, 256–257

Rules, 124–125, 159, 205, 209, 231

S

Sample Circles, 266

Sampling Dots and Beads (lesson), 173–179

Sampling to Understand Populations: agendas for, 173, 180–181, 186; discussions from, 176, 182–184, 188–189; exploration in, 175–176, 188; extensions for, 184; launches for, 174–175, 182, 187–188; look-fors from, 176–177, 184–185, 189–190; play in, 182–183; reflections from, 177, 185, 190; for teachers, 174, 181–182, 187

Scaling measurements: big ideas for, 47–49; data and, 81; drawings and, 52; intuition for, 56; multiplication from, 99–100; reflections

on, 53, 58, 67; solids for, 61; for students, 73–74, 76

Science. *See* Neuroscience

Seeing Proportional Relationships, 69–71, 91; agendas for, 72–73, 80, 86–87; discussions from, 75, 82, 88–89; exploration in, 74, 88; extensions for, 75; launches for, 73–74, 81, 87; look-fors from, 75–76, 82–83, 89–90; reflections from, 76, 84, 90; for teachers, 73, 81, 87

Seeing Slices (lesson), 29–33

Shapes, 27, 29, 37

Simple Spinner, 121–122, 126

Situations, 93–94, 109, 112, 177

Size, 180

Sizing Up Proportions, 86, 91

Sizing Up Proportions (lesson), 86–91

Skepticism, 8

Sketching, 32, 32–33, 57

Skill, 122–123, 135

Slice Hypotheses Sheet, 36, 39

Slope, 69–71, 73

Small object collections, 19

Smith, Leon Polk, 153–154

Snap Cube Grid Paper, 276

Snap cubes, 18, 61, 63–64, 276

Solids, 30–31, 33, 35, 37–38, 41, 61–64

Spinner 1, 121–122, 127

Spinner 2, 121–122, 128

Spinner 3, 121–122, 129

Spinner 4, 121–122, 130

Square prisms, 42

Square tiles, 18

Squares, 261–262

Stanford University, 3–4, 9–10, 268

Statistics, 171–172

Strategies: discussions of, 173, 208; for documentation, 190; observations and, 176, 210; rules and, 124–125; for students, 123, 159; for tasks, 176–177; variation and, 189

Stress, 2

Strogatz, Steve, 226–227

Students: accuracy by, 66, 114, 184–185, 188; adding machine tape for, 104, 110; ambiguity for, 37–38; approximations by, 264, 271; brainstorming by, 87; challenges for, 88; communication between, 190; confidence of, 139, 182; conjectures by, 41–42, 139; connections by, 115, 148, 160; creativity of, 56, 134, 158–159, 165,